Justified anger

Why Productive Americans Are So Angry

Roger P. Bolton

ISBN: 1463584598
ISBN-13: 9781463584597

TABLE OF CONTENTS

FOREWORD

There is a time for healthy people to be angry and to express that anger, and the time is now. Productive Americans have been used and abused by our government for a long time, but especially in the last three years as the results and rewards of our hard work have been taken from us by politicians and given to those who have done nothing to deserve them. We have been slow getting to this place, but the escalating events of the past three years have hit us in the face with what politicians have been doing to us for decades.

Many of us have been brought to the realization that the legislators and presidents in Washington have set us on a course, if not corrected, will lead to the destruction of the greatest nation in the history of the world. Our Constitution was set up for government to serve the people. It seems now that the Constitution is nothing more than a historical curiosity to the people who walk the halls of Congress. Politicians are doing their best to make people serve government, communicating to citizens that they have every right to use and abuse us as they see fit. Politicians are gradually taking away our freedoms with laws which allow incursion into all areas of our lives.

If productive people were not angry about what politicians have been doing in Washington for many years, it would indicate that we are not in touch with what it means to be a healthy, free people.

Productive people are also angry at what politicians have done to poor people, many of them our neighbors, for it has generated the environment where many think it is okay to take from the productive and give to the unproductive. If poor people could figure out what politicians have done and are doing to them, they, too, would be angry, but they have not yet seen through how politicians are keeping them poor and subservient to serve their own ends.

One of the worst things that can be done for the mental health of people is to remove from them the responsibility of taking care of themselves. The government has done an effective job in convincing millions of Americans that their future is guaranteed by feeding at the trough in Washington, and they have become dependent on the monthly "gov'ment" check. Mental health professionals use the diagnosis, "Dependent Personality Disorder," in referring to those who are overly dependent on others for their care. This is a deep and pervasive need to be taken care of by another, which leads to total dependence on the other, sometimes going to the point where life cannot continue without that person. This definition exactly fits those individuals healthy enough to work who have chosen to accept the "gov'ment" check and remove themselves from being productive citizens. We all know that this government trough is provided by politicians taking money from the pockets of productive people.

What many people do not realize is that dependency is a two-way street. Where one is dependent on another, the other is also dependent. They both cannot get along without each other. The welfare recipient must have those who give to them, and those who give to them, primarily the democrats, must have the poor to give to.

Politicians know, if they have any intelligence at all, it is not good for millions of people to be idle and contribute nothing to the well-being of our country, but something is far more important to them than the well-being of our country, and that something is getting re-elected. This is what has caused so much damage to the United States, and is part of what makes productive people so angry. Politicians have sacrificed the good of our nation for their own enhancement.

PREFACE

Quality of life in the United States has taken a significant hit in the last three years. Deterioration has been taking place for a number of years, but it has accelerated during the current administration.

We face the very real threat that this will get even worse in the next few months if significant changes are not made. The power structure in Washington has now taken the position that government can force anything, good or bad, on American citizens, requiring us to do anything they decide we should do. This was particularly evident in the ill-conceived healthcare legislation and the stupefying $800 billion bail-out program shoved down our throats by politicians having no idea what they were doing. When Ms. Pelosi said, "Let's pass it so we can see what is in it," she said loud and clear that Congress and the president care little about what a majority of Americans think and want. The rhetoric from the oval office is replete with the desire to control the lives of the American people. We are now threatened with a loss of freedom to be and do what we wish that is unparalleled in our history, and, if politicians have their way, we will lose that which has led the world to envy the way of life we have built in the United States.

It does not surprise well-informed people that this current unrest and dissatisfaction with our government in Washington is so great among productive people. It is far greater than during the Korean War, the Vietnam War, the economic troubles during the Carter administration, even during the civil rights struggle, and, if the current power structure remains in Washington, this unrest will get worse.

The belief among people this author knows is that politicians in Washington for many years have lost sight of what has made America great, and lack understanding regarding what they are supposed to do as elected officials. During the last three years in particular, failure of politicians to represent a majority of the American people in legislative decisions has reached a new and sinister level. This has happened because we have come more and more under the control of men and women who have nowhere else to go for wisdom than their own minds and each other.

Most productive people believe the Obama administration has plans to replace our constitutional government with national socialism of some kind while having no idea what that form of socialism will be. To the detriment of the entire nation, our public educational system teaches socialism, this by teachers and professors who lack an understanding and appreciation of the value of freedom to choose what we do with our lives. Rather than being educated, our students are being indoctrinated to believe the State can do more for them than they can do for themselves. Socialism can never give to people the opportunity to dream big dreams and then follow those dreams. The marvelous achievements of the United States could never have happened under socialism. If the current group of liberals/socialists/communists now in power in Washington have their way, we will become nothing more than a shell of the nation we once were. When this writer compares the people of today with those who pulled themselves up out of the Great Depression and became, in Tom Brokaw's words, "The Greatest Generation," the word "wimps" best suits contemporary Americans.

For a long time, politicians seem to have believed they have been endowed with ultimate knowledge and wisdom when they cross the Potomac River, having become capable of solving every problem known to mankind. Many of us voters see them as bumbling clowns incapable of making decisions regarding what is best for all Americans. If we examine closely the many things they have done, too many of them can be labeled "bad for America." When set against our freedoms and the guidelines of the Constitution, much of what they do simply does not make good sense, giving no indication that they are products of rational minds. Irrationality is perhaps a good word to use in relation to many of the things they do. This is the price we have paid for sending people to Washington who have no idea of their need for something beyond their own wisdom.

Although we deplore many things done by politicians during the past 60 years, we have hope, and that hope is in the opportunity to return to the basis of what has made us such a great nation. We still have a vote and can put people back in Washington who understand we became great through the initiative and accomplishments of people given freedom to pursue their own dreams, not through the initiative and dreams of politicians.

No effort is made to minimize the shortcomings and failures of our nation. We know we will never solve all our problems simply because we are human beings. Our task is not to hide our heads in the sand or develop programs which make things worse, as is often done in Washington. It is to work on solving problems as we are able, while learning, to better involve all our people in pursuit of personal achievement. Throwing out the baby with the bath water will not bring solutions to our problems; it will only compound them.

During the last three years, we have seen a steady stream of lies, discrimination, bribery, deceit, blaming of others for personal failures, and other things which indicate a fundamental misunderstanding of our Constitution, Bill of Rights, and general responsibility to provide an environment which encourages us all to be a part of moving our freedoms forward.

It is ironic that so many people the world over are struggling to enjoy the freedoms we Americans enjoy, as illustrated by the vast numbers immigrating to our country, and, also, the cry for freedom that is going on in the Middle East, while at the same time many politicians in Washington are attempting to replace our form of government with a form which makes us subservient to their whims and limitations, one which takes our freedoms from us.

CHAPTER ONE

THE AMERICA I GREW UP IN

The Great Depression was raging when I came into the world. Mama and five of us children lived on $25 a month plus chickens in the yard and a cow Grandpa let us milk for free. At age four I picked cotton as well as split all the wood my mama used in the cook stove in the winter of 1938-39. The house we lived in had only outside, airy walls, a roof with no ceiling, and a wooden floor through which we could see the dirt underneath. In cold weather, if we were not close to the fireplace, we were about as cold as if we had been outside. When it rained, the roof leaked. Sometimes the only thing we had to eat in the house was cornbread and buttermilk (and I still like it today). There is no question about it; we were poor.

WE WERE BORN INTO A CONSTITUTIONAL REPUBLIC

As a kid, I had no idea what a "constitutional republic" was. In fact, it must have been my teenage years before I even heard the phrase. Once I began to study history and learn why our form of government is so different from those of other nations, it began to dawn on me just how special life here can be.

My family did not remain poor. We learned early on that hard work and education would give us an opportunity to elevate ourselves above where we had been. We found that, when we diligently applied ourselves, there was no barrier to what we could do, and there was no limitation on how far we could go in life. What happened in our lives was up to us. There was no religion, no government, no anything other than ourselves that could give us life. It was entirely up to us.

When I began to learn about the beginnings of our country, set against the backdrop of the history of other nations where people were subservient to government, it slowly dawned on me that freedom to make of my life what I wanted it to be was extraordinary. There is no record in recorded history of anything quite like this. I lived in a special country!

Of course, we have struggled with freedom being available to all, but we have managed to make progress in overcoming the human condition of taking advantage of each other. As a republic, under the wisdom of our people as a whole, we can continue our course of providing freedom for all. This is a promise not possible in any other form of government.

William Gladstone, the four-time Prime Minister of England, once said the Constitution of the United States was "the most wonderful work ever struck off at a given time by the brain and purpose of man." This was a miraculous document, and many countries around the world have used it as a guide in forming their own governments.

The ultimate power of a nation being placed in the hands of citizens is unprecedented, but that is what the Constitution does for us. I grew up with the understanding that my government was answerable to me and everyone else, and would be working for my benefit.

One of the magnificent contributions of George Washington was his refusal to be king. When our government was being formed, he received the suggestion that he be referred to as "His Excellency." He wanted nothing of this because he was aware that a king has tyrannical powers over the people. He and the other framers of our nation gave us a republic in which the government derives all its power from the people, doing only those things that are acceptable to those who are governed. Ultimate authority belongs in the people alone. In a republic, the State cannot force its citizens to do things that are against their will. This is quite clear in our founding documents.

I was born in this country and grew up with a government which served my needs. With very few exceptions, politicians in Washington provided an environment in which I could rise to a level determined only by me. For the most part, they have honored and followed the Constitution. As a result, my life has been far more rewarding, complete and enjoyable than had they set my course.

WE HAD FREEDOM TO CHOOSE

In reviewing my life, I did nothing which could not have been done by anyone with a good mind and a determination to succeed. True, there were circumstances in the lives of others more problematic than mine, but there are too many stories of less fortunate people becoming far more successful than me to believe anyone could not have made a good life. My best friend in elementary school in South Georgia chose to quit school in the eleventh grade, giving up on education, and, therefore, guaranteeing a less than satisfactory life of achievement for himself and his personal family. Too many people, some I work with, have ended their quest for achievement even before they have gotten a good start, but it has been there and they have turned their backs on it. For those without a high school diploma, the GED is there for the taking with a little work, and additional education beyond that awaits them, but it is rare when one who quits school decides to go back and prepare for a better life.

In the hospitals where I was CEO, we had programs to reimburse employees for attending school to better prepare themselves for the future, making it possible for them to get better jobs and earn more money. In not one hospital was there one employee on the lower end of the economic scale who took advantage of this. It was those who already had academic achievement who pursued additional education. It was there for everyone, but those with the least income never accessed it. Perhaps poor people remain poor because being poor is more than the community in which they live; it is, in many respects, a condition of the mind.

The "Greatest Generation" came through the tough times, but understood something of the greatness of America and were willing to die for its preservation. They won the Second World War, came home and built the most fantastic economy and nation ever to appear on the face of the earth. We struggled with many things as some of our people tried their best to continue and/or impose limitations on certain segments of our population, but we found more ways to extend freedom to additional people, a process which will never be totally complete because human beings have a tendency to elevate themselves at the expense of others.

We worked hard and we played hard in order to make our way. It was rare to see a fat person, and I never saw an obese person until I was in my latter years of high school. Our work habits and discipline kept us active, and we just did not gorge ourselves with food we did not need. I never knew of anyone without a job turning down the offer of a job, no matter what it paid. This happens all the time now because too many people are satisfied with the inadequate "gov'ment" check, and many of the "poor people" are the most obese people in the country.

One of the things causing me and my generation to feel good about ourselves was recognition of achievement. If we did well, we were rewarded for our efforts. The star I received every day in first grade for brushing my teeth and bringing a clean handkerchief helped me feel good about myself and gave me motivation to do well in other things. Reward has been a hallmark of our capitalistic system, and has been a primary motivation for people to sacrifice and work hard. Out of this has come achievements in academia, athletics, science, industry, the business world or any other endeavor one might mention. The rewards have been there for effort and success. The best basketball player, baseball player, football player, business leader, etc., etc. earns the most money. This is the way it ought to be, because, without reward for those who do well, people tend to slack off and not try. I have been recipient of some rewards, and they have motivated me to do better.

We did not expect a free ride. Motivation, discipline and achievement were three things honored in about every area of life. It was understood that achievement and enjoyment of the good life could not be realized without discipline. We learned to expect good grades only if we put time into study. We learned receipt of gold stars came only after we earned them. Sometimes we did not receive what we thought we had earned, but this gave us motivation to try a little harder. If we stuck to things, rewards would come our way. We did not complain about being discriminated against when we did not get what we thought we should have.

As we pursue the freeing-up of individuals in the future to build their lives on their own personal dreams, not on things imposed by other people or government, we will find an explosion of achievement and accomplishment as people open up their lives to develop what is on the inside of them. As this progressively happens, the benefits of freedom will expand and grow, and the greatness of our nation will increase.

There will never be a greater nation than the United States, and we will never again rise to that greatness with what is going on in Washington. In curtailing our march toward freedom for all to determine their own way in life, we are letting other nations take up the gauntlet of offering more freedom to its people. Any one person, party or group of people who wish to replace what we now have in America with any other form of government will be taking us backward toward the loss of freedom and the limitations which lack of freedom imposes on people.

In order for people to reach the highest level of achievement their talents and efforts will allow, they must be given freedom to pursue their own dreams, not the dreams of anyone else, and especially not the dreams of politicians. We must find ways to expand, not curtail, freedom for all our people. This flies in the face of what many politicians want for our citizens.

WE WERE FREE TO GO WHERE WE WANTED TO GO AND BUY WHAT WE COULD AFFORD

When I was a poor kid in South Georgia, living 12 miles from town, my mother would occasionally let a brother and me go to town when she went on her monthly trip to buy a few staples. At times, when available, she would give us a nickel to spend, and we could buy anything we desired costing no more than five cents. At times, we would buy a Baby Ruth, but most of the time we would head for the creamery and buy a double-dip ice cream cone. Oh!!!, was that ever good!!! - and only five cents!!!

We could purchase anything this nickel could buy. This is in contrast to other countries where there was no nickel or items on shelves for people to buy. I remember the stories and pictures coming out of communist USSR of the bare shelves in stores even when people had money to spend, and of poor countries where they did not even have stores. Even during the Great Depression, stores in the U.S. had the basic needs of people. This was not the case in other countries. I have never known of the unavailability in America of anything I wanted except during World War Two, and then I had everything I needed. I may not have had the money, but what was needed was there. The bubble gum I wanted was not available, but I did not need it.

Nobody made me buy anything, and, if it was available, nobody kept me from buying it if I had the money.

Freedom to go anywhere desired has been a great benefit to Americans. Not only have we been able to go anywhere in the United States that struck our fancy, but, with a passport in hand, we could go just about anywhere in the world we desired. No-one in this country placed limitations on us. This has not been so in many other parts of the world. The image that comes to mind is of the Berlin wall separating and confining people, not allowing them to go where they desired. Right now, I could go to England, Australia, South Africa, India or most other countries of the world, and I would have to ask no-one for permission to go, just purchase my ticket and go with passport in hand.

Many Americans have not understood the blessings freedom has brought to us. Just recently, a couple of missionaries were asking for gifts of towels, bath cloths and other linens because there was none available where they served. In much of the world even the basic necessities of life are non-existent. People have not been free to pursue their own dreams because they have lived under governments controlled by people who have no idea what freedom is all about, and the potential and possibilities that lie deep within the minds and souls of their people. Our form of government has provided this for us.

WE WERE CHARITABLE

The people of the United States as a whole have given more to charity than any other nation in history. Our religions have encouraged us to be charitable, and even non-religious people have felt the desire to give where there is need. And, of course, in order to give, one must have money to give. Our capitalistic system has created an economy in which we have within our hands enough money for ourselves plus some to give away. And, amazingly, the biggest percentage givers live in the State of Mississippi, the poorest state in the nation. We seem to have a sense that to be blessed should lead us to bless the lives of those in need.

The big givers like Bill and Melinda Gates, Warren Buffet, and Ted Turner make the headlines, giving because they have achieved great wealth in our economy, but it is those with average incomes who make up the bulk of our donations. As a small giver, I am proud to be a part of a great economy which provides me with enough money to donate to worthy causes.

Many foundations have been funded by people who have amassed fortunes in our great economy, and funds from these foundations meet many needs, primarily in this country, but in some other countries as well. In 2008, during the worst economic climate since the Great Depression, charitable giving totaled $307.65 billion. Americans are a giving people, and it is made possible by our outstanding economy and the caring hearts of our people.

Only a free market society can produce what we have produced. When people realize they have been gifted by their Creator to produce beyond their needs and are responsible to him for what they do with what they have, they become a charitable people. You cannot recognize your responsibility to God and his creation and be a Scrooge. Many people around the world have nothing to give, but in America we have enjoyed much more than we need. The combination of money in our hands and knowledge of responsibility to God and to each other will always lead to charity. Our economy and our faith have made it possible to be the biggest giving nation in history.

WE ENJOYED FREEDOM OF RELIGION

From my earliest memories, attending church has been a part of my life. As I grew, there were those who wanted to box me in with certain beliefs, but I found the freedom to build my faith on my own thinking and experiences. Had I chosen, I could have changed my religion or not had any religion at all. The climate in this country provided me with freedom to build my religion any way I wanted.

Religious freedom is not possible in many countries. Too often, we hear and see reports of people being disowned, punished or even murdered when they fail to be faithful to the religion in which they grew up. Not long ago I watched a video clandestinely made as a teenage girl was stoned to death because she violated a religious law. This amounts to religious terrorism and slavery because it denies people the opportunity to work out their own beliefs. There is no religious freedom at all in certain parts of the world as clerics and others impose their will upon people, claiming to be speaking the very words of their God.

History is full of efforts to deny people freedom of religion. We need only refer to the Christian Crusades or the Inquisition or the cry of radical Muslims to "kill the satanic Americans" to be reminded of the devastation which comes when people desire to force religion upon people. One of the reasons many of the first settlers came to the United States was to gain freedom of religion, something not available in England and other countries at that time.

There are some religious leaders in our country who would like to use legislation to impose their beliefs on others. Their intention may or may not be good, but, in a society offering freedom of religion, we cannot impose our beliefs on each other. If we fail to maintain freedom of religion for everyone, there could come a time when a religion foreign to our own would be able to impose their beliefs on our practices. We may already be seeing the beginnings of this, so it is vitally important that we hold on to religious freedom for all.

WE WERE SAFE AND WE HELPED EACH OTHER

When living in South Georgia, I never heard any discussion about the possibility of being unsafe in our community. We did not lock our doors for fear of a break-in, and when we went anywhere there was nothing said about people wanting to take things belonging to us. When we moved to Atlanta in late 1942, we were one of four white families in a black community, and there was never any expression from my parents about any fear of living there. A few years later in West End, living adjacent to a poor community, my mother walked home in the dark after getting off the bus from her job in downtown Atlanta, and we never had thoughts about danger she might face between the trolley and our front door.

The ability to choose what to do with our lives is a gift of our Constitution and Bill of Rights. It is a necessary part of a free society, and it is this from which our greatness has sprung. If we follow the Constitution, we will recognize that bringing hurt to others limits not only them, but ourselves as well. As a nation, we understood this much better than people seem to at the present time.

A good society will produce people who have respect for each other, and where there is respect there is safety. I was privileged to be in a family which saw each individual as a gift of God, and, as such, deserved to be treated with dignity and respect. Oh yes, there were times when we failed each other and caused unnecessary grief, but we would always remember who we were and where we came from.

Even on the farms in South Georgia in the late 1930's and the 1940's I saw respect from both whites and blacks. Blacks and whites worked side-by-side in the tobacco fields and at the tobacco barn, and I never witnessed disrespect. We all worked together to get our jobs done, and people were paid the same regardless of their color. I remember cropping tobacco beside a kind, elderly black gentleman, and being amazed that he could tell the time of day without owning a watch. He told me he could do this just by observing the position of the sun. I thought he was something, and he returned the favor.

Coming out of the Great Depression and World War Two, politicians were aware of the sacrifices of "The Greatest Generation" (description by Tom Brokaw), and developed programs to encourage and support people in their quest to build good lives. Out of this came the opportunity for individuals to develop and pursue their own dreams. Barriers to success for a majority of our people were almost non-existent, and we built the strongest economy ever to exist. People I knew were optimistic about the future because the future was in our hands, not in the hands of politicians. Our future would become what we made it. We and many politicians understood certain things were necessary if success was to be ours, things like study and hard work. Coming out of the Depression and world war, we were not afraid to work, seeing in it our opportunity to provide an ever increasing better life for ourselves and our loved ones. As a result of this, millions the world over clamored more and more to become a part of our nation so they could participate in building their own success.

Although politicians have often gotten in the way of individual success and achievement, the ones in my early years were predominantly eager to support the efforts of people to improve their lot in life. There were some less than desirable politicians in office then, but most of them seemed to appreciate their role of supporting people in their efforts to be successful, not in controlling what people thought and did.

There were and still are many things needing to be done to involve all citizens in opportunities for achievement, but the successes we had in building our nation made it possible for us to address some of our weaknesses.

With the government supporting its people, and the people working together in their quest for success, it was only a matter of time until we built an economy the likes of which had never before been seen anywhere in the world.

The America I grew up in opened the future for me to become what I wanted to become. My success depended upon me, and, even though there have been those who have sought to diminish my life, where I have been and what I have done has been entirely up to me. It has often not been easy, but the good life was there for the taking if I had the grit and determination to go after it. This great nation extended this freedom to me, and, as I review my life, I would not swap it with anyone. It has been the life I built. There is no-one who could have given me a better life than me.

POLITICIANS WERE HELPING AMERICANS SUCCEED

When I grew up, it seems everyone around me was interested in my success, not from the standpoint of what I could do for them, but what I could do for myself. In my particular environment, the emphasis was not on building great wealth, but on building a great life. It was understood, in order for me to do this, I would have to do my own pushing, and, if I pushed in the right direction and hard enough, success would be mine. As a result, I prepared myself, getting more education and training than the average person, and I have enjoyed a good life.

Not only did encouragement come from my individual environment, but it came from the environment of my entire country, with the very center of the thrust for me to do well being in the government in Washington. Politicians knew if I succeeded, along with other Americans, we could have a great country. Politicians encouraged my success.

The American story, fueled by the dreams of our Founding Fathers, has enabled us to move away from government controlled by kings, princes, clerics and others who subjugate people for their own ends. Although we have had setbacks to our march toward freedom for all our citizens, we have, none-the-less, been on our way.

Yes, I had to pay my taxes, but, in the first three decades of my life, I did not object because, in spite of some of the shenanigans of dysfunctional politicians in Washington, I felt they were, as a whole, wanting to continue building a nation of freedom for all. I felt good about the road we were on because I felt politicians were cheering me to be successful and build a good life.

We have had many struggles as a nation, and our politicians have helped us get through them. So long as they do the right things, a part of which is providing an environment that encourages us to do the right things, we will continue to build the kind of nation our Founders dreamed about.

CHAPTER TWO

THE AMERICA I NOW LIVE IN

The America I now live in is not close to being what it once was. We are a people and a government who have chosen to move away from some of the fundamental things which have made us great. All around me I see things no-one in the 1950'S and 1960's could have dreamed would ever be true in this country.

MOTIVATION & ACHIEVEMENT: A THING OF THE PAST

In many places we have abandoned emphasis on motivation and achievement. A speaker I heard a few months ago said his son has 22 awards for involvement in sports and other activities. The speaker told his son he had seven awards from when he was young. Then he asked his son how many of those awards had he won, and the son told him he had won five. He told his son he had won all seven of his. His son had been given awards just for participation, and he told about one individual receiving an award who never came to the activities, but had only signed up. Discipline and achievement had nothing to do with receiving an award. This is all too prevalent in our society; you don't have to do anything to receive awards. This is a true killer of discipline and opportunities for achievement, thus removing people from any sense of the need to work hard in order to be successful. The biggest culprit in this is the federal government as many handout programs give millions of people a monthly check for doing nothing.

WELFARE: GUARANTEED POVERTY

Last year, in one of the classes I facilitate, an attractive and seemingly intelligent woman in her mid to late 30's reported having been on welfare for a long number of years, and on two occasions said, "Welfare is guaranteed poverty." After coming to approximately eight classes, she told class members she was going to get a job. Class members complemented her for this. Two weeks later, she told the class she had been offered a job, but, "I don't know if I'm going to accept it." The following week, she advised the class she was not going to take the job. When asked ,"Why?," she said, "Because it pays only a little more than my welfare check." Class members said to her, "Can't you see this is a stepping stone to a better job, and you will be able to make a better life for yourself and your family?" She did not take the job. The federal government, through welfare and other give-away programs, has killed the motivation and, thus, achievement of this lady and millions of other people in this country, and, during the last two years this has picked up speed. When fully capable people choose to be cared for by the government, they, over time, lose their determination and skills to take care of themselves. Just as you lose the skills of a muscle if you do not use it, so you lose the skills of self-care if you turn things over to others or the government. Additionally, people do not have to use their minds in order to receive money from the government, so they lose much of their ability to know what to do with the potential in their lives.

Welfare has indeed been needed by some, but, by giving capable people money for doing nothing, it has taken millions of people off the job market and resulted in them contributing nothing to the betterment of our nation. In effect, it has made good people into useless people who are a drag on our entire nation. The latest statistics I could get my hands on (March, 2011) show the following:

8% of the population, 29 million, are on welfare. Of these:

39% are white

38% are black

17% are Hispanic

Cost of the Welfare program: $29 billion.

Medicaid statistics are as follows:

50 million are on Medicaid

Cost is $273 billion

Food stamps: 40 million people at a cost of $70 billion.

So far, I have met no-one who begrudges truly needy people receiving any of the above assistance. What galls many productive people, those who pay taxes which support these programs, is the receipt of assistance by those who are fully capable of working, but who have chosen to be lazy and become wards of the government.

Many people tell me stories like one I observed at a local grocery store. I stepped into the check-out lane as a lady in far better clothes than I have ever owned paid for things in her grocery cart. She put all the groceries on the conveyor belt and paid for them with food stamps. She then put the alcohol on the conveyor belt and paid for it with a $100 bill. She went on out and I paid for my few items. When I got to the parking lot, she was putting her things into an obviously new Cadillac Escalade. Because of the time of day and the way she was dressed, she probably had just gotten off a well-paying job. If this was an isolated incident, productive people would pay little attention to it, but everyone I have told about this has said they see the same thing. We tax-payers are having money extracted from our pockets by the government in Washington to support this kind of dishonesty and theft by fully capable people. Some people would say that legislators who developed such an easily abused system were not very bright; some would even use the word "stupid."

In a recent editorial in the Atlanta Journal/Constitution, one of the editorial writers decried the suggestion that people receiving any form of welfare should report and justify their need for government assistance once per year. A check and balance system is reasonable, and would go a long way toward catching those who, like the lady above, are obvious cheaters. The editorial writer said we should just trust people. How absurd!!! Any system without checks and balances will be abused by participants. We all know this, well, perhaps not politicians and government employees. History has shown that many people will not be responsible if they are not required to be responsible.

As previously suggested, because of the availability of governmental assistance programs, many people have not prepared themselves to do anything, and, as a result, have no skills with which to get a job. Through the disastrous mortgage program of the past few years, which allowed people to purchase homes with no income and no evidence of ability to pay a mortgage note, quite a number of homes in my middle class neighborhood were purchased by welfare people right out of government housing. Two houses side-by-side were occupied by people who had no idea they had the responsibility of home ownership. The grass grew to over belt high before they finally figured out it would not be cut by the government; it wouldn't be done unless they did it themselves. Of course, the leaves, shrubs and other things did not get attention for well over a year. In addition, neither family paid the mortgage, and each house has been in foreclosure at least six times. One family finally moved out, and the house has now been up for auction over one year. Eight years ago, this house was worth $250,000. If it sells at auction for more than $60,000, it will be a surprise.

The above are clear examples of why productive people are so angry. We have been hurt by a government which has taken an increasing amount of tax money out of our pockets and given to non-productive people for doing absolutely nothing, and there does not seem to be an end to this being done. While more and more money has been removed from our pockets by the government, the value of our property has declined by 40 to 75 percent because of the mortgage mess made by members of congress. Citizens did nothing to bring this about. It was forced on us by irresponsible politicians in Washington.

Following some legislation Bill Clinton signed, he made the comment, "This will end poverty as we know it." He was absolutely right. It took poverty right out of the slums and deposited it in thousands of middle class neighborhoods like mine, and it has ruined these neighborhoods. People came out of the slums, but the slums did not come out of the people. Life in the slums of this country is often not about the houses people live in; it's about the slums that live in people. That's why there are now five abandoned houses within five hundred yards of where I live, two houses up for foreclosure multiple times within rock throwing distance, and lifestyles previously found only in slum housing.

It is abundantly clear that governmental handout programs severely limit the freedom of individuals to develop their talents and abilities and pursue the best in life only available through achievement. Government programs trap people in a life of poverty and uselessness. When people are paid for doing nothing or given things they have not earned, life for them becomes inferior to what it could be if they diligently developed and applied the good things they have on the inside. When politicians do for people what they should do for themselves, life may get better for a few, but the majority of us have the quality of our lives diminished.

The irrationality of politicians gave us the welfare programs, and this same irrationality undergirds their continuance. It does not make sense that capable people are encouraged to turn their backs on productive lives, and then receive monthly checks for doing absolutely nothing. People have the right to choose to live worthless lives and receive the fruits of worthlessness, but the politicians in Washington are committing legalized theft by forcing taxpayers to fund this waste of human potential.

WELFARE: THE BREEDING GROUND OF CRIME

It was no surprise that crime skyrocketed when welfare people moved into my county. That was to be expected because welfare produces crime. Just last evening, approximately 1.5 miles from my home, there was a home invasion in which three people were shot. Then, a few minutes ago, WSB in Atlanta reported that a manager of Fred's, approximately four miles from my home was robbed and shot in the leg when he was taking a deposit to the bank. Police are now looking for a young man in dreadlocks. Not long after this, I was told about a drive-by shooting. It is probably safe to say that these perpetrators came from welfare families.

In June, 1995, Michael Tanner, Director of Health and Welfare Studies, Cato Institute, made a speech before the Subcommittee on Youth Violence, Committee on the Judiciary, United States Senate, and referenced a report by the Maryland NAACP, which stated, "…the ready access to a lifetime of welfare and free social service programs is a major contributory factor to the crime problems we face today." Mr. Tanner also referenced research by Dr. June O'Neal and Anne Hill for the U. S. Department of Health and Human services "…showed that a 50 percent increase in the monthly value of combined AFDC and food stamp benefits led to a 117 percent increase in the crime rate among young black men" (information taken from the internet).

Many other sources of information confirm the above: **welfare and other government give-away programs are a direct genesis of crime in the United States.** This is what politicians in Washington have done to welfare people because of their belief that poor people are incapable of caring for themselves unless the government sends them "free money," but also what they have done to productive people because they have had to confiscate this "free money" out of the pockets of those who have worked hard to earn it. And, with these welfare criminals being everywhere, now in our previously good communities, all of us face heightened danger from them.

What this amounts to is our politicians have developed programs to finance crime in this country. They, in an attempt to "take care of the poor," are providing the environment, using my money and that of other taxpayers, where individuals with no purpose in life have time to plan and rob those who have worked hard to succeed. As verbalized by the lady who said, "Welfare is guaranteed poverty," welfare money is not enough to provide people with the kind of living they desire, so the stress is there for them to take what does not belong to them.

A sad commentary in this entire welfare mess is that many politicians want it this way. It is the only way they can guarantee votes at the next election.

By making poor people depend on the government check for housing, food, clothing, transportation, health insurance, even cell phones, etc., these people have no choice but to vote for those who will give them more. And, the politicians must give them more and more for the poor to vote for them. Both depend on the other for life tomorrow.

GOVERNMENT: DESTROYING FAMILIES

The following story appeared on television yesterday. A married couple with two children did not have their preferred income. They learned about the government program available to single mothers in which the single mother could apply for and receive government assistance. So, what did this couple do? They got a divorce, and she applied for and began receiving a government check because she was a single mother. But, the "former" husband did not move out. Their life continued as it had been. They had snookered the government because the politicians had set up a program which was easily snookered. This program, in and of itself, has communicated to men that the women they impregnate will be better off if they disappear. This removes from them any sense of being responsible for the children they father. This is one of the primary reasons the man at church could tell of working with a bunch of kids near Fulton County Stadium in Atlanta, stating that 100 percent of these children did not live with both parents, and 75 percent lived with neither parent. This is the work of politicians who fail to place emphasis on being responsible for what we do.

This program is indicative of the intelligence level of the lawmakers we have sent to Washington to make this a better nation for all citizens. It is clear indication of the irrationality that pervades Washington. A sad reality is that many politicians want to develop more programs similar to this one where capable people are sucked into a life of dependency. Other programs similar to this are destroying our country.

WE ARE NOW A FAILING NATION

In my estimation, the decline of our nation during the last 80 years, stretching all the way back to FDR's social security program, has made us significantly weaker than we were when I grew up. As an example, we have millions of farmers who cannot find the labor needed to harvest their crops while millions more people receive the "gov'ment" check for doing nothing. As a result, the producers of our food have hired illegal aliens to get the work done, and would like to hire more. The government is sending monthly checks to people who should be out in the fields earning a living, but who are home doing nothing. This sort of thing would never have happened in the America I grew up in when we would take any legal job, regardless of what it paid, just to put food on the table for our families.

Some people present themselves as too good to work for wages which are not up to their standards. The gentleman in my class lost his $15 an hour job. Shortly thereafter, he was offered a job making $7.50 per hour. He told class members, "I am not going to take a job making so much less than what I was making." Class members tried to help him understand that he could still be looking for another job while making $7.50 an hour. In so many words, he let them know that this was beneath his dignity. It took him a little over six months to find a job with an hourly rate satisfactory to him. When he told class members about the new job, they reminded him that he could have made a total of $7,800 while he was waiting for better pay.

What we need to do is stop sending welfare checks to healthy, capable people. Then we would have more Americans working on farms and less need for illegal aliens. It would make things easier for farmers, and would cause lazy, non-productive people to get up and do something worthwhile for our country or go hungry.

If our legislators in Washington had read and understood the Constitution of the United States and had been diligent students of history, we would never have reached a time when eight percent of our population could make it only if the government removed more and more tax money from the pockets of productive Americans. Our nation, based on the foundation of our Constitution, has become the envy of the world, with countless foreigners clamoring to come here for a better life. Many of our so-called "poor people" are far better off than poor people of other countries, so it is no wonder many people want to come here.

It is crazy that Obama and his people, many of them having gotten wealthy in our capitalistic system, wish now to replace what we have with national socialism. The impact of what they have done in the past two years will trouble us for many years as we work our way back to the basic foundation of our nation.

The communication, "I/we can make a better way for you than you can make for yourself," a communication getting louder and louder from Washington, speaks loud and clear to the failure of politicians to recognize that the source of our greatness is the ability of individuals to make their own way in building their lives free from unreasonable encroachments by their government.

One of the things becoming more of a problem is the failure of politicians to recognize something firmly stated by our Founding Fathers in the Declaration of Independence: "We hold these truths to be self-evident, that all men are created equal, that they are endowed by their Creator with certain unalienable rights, that among these are Life, Liberty and pursuit of Happiness." They have turned their backs on one of the things of primary importance to those who laid the foundation of our great nation. Their laws and programs of the last 80 years have too often been based on their belief that people lack the ability to take care of themselves, and need government to do for them what they should be doing for themselves. One of the things often heard by successful athletic teams competing for championships is something like this: "Stick to what 'brung' (brought) you here." Recognition of God has been one of the many things which has brought us to being a successful nation, and we need to stick with it.

As already fully stated, politicians have often developed many programs for the purpose of securing (or buying) votes for the next election. They have even gone so far as to bribe people and organizations in order to secure their votes, as was abundantly clear when the democrats bribed the unions to secure their positive support for Obama Care. Then, many of us older people were chagrined when AARP leadership supported the bill. It came out later that this leadership accepted millions of dollars from the democrats to support a bill which removed $500 billion from Medicare. And, we have since learned that AARP is receiving an exemption for part of the healthcare bill. This was and is nothing other than acceptance of a bribe. Not only did they bribe organizations and unions, but they also had to bribe members of their own party to get them to vote for it. Had it not been for these bribes given by Obama and the democrats, the healthcare bill would never have been passed.

Any piece of legislation which cannot stand on its own merit, as was true of the healthcare legislation, and many others, should not be put into law. We have seen this happen again and again as lies have been told, threats have been made, bribes have been given, and laws passed without members of congress having read them, i. e., Obama Care. These sorts of things constitute abandonment of the democratic process, and are at the heart of much of the anger on the part of people who pay taxes. To hear one of the democratic leaders say, "Let's vote and pass the bill, and then we can find out what's in it," is abject absurdity, and speaks loud and clear to the fact that intelligence and reason often are not part of the legislative agenda in Washington.

If we continue the agenda of the last few years, we, as a nation, will become weaker and weaker, not resembling the great nation we once were.

WE ARE NOW LOSING FREEDOM OF RELIGION

The First Amendment to the United States Constitution states, "Congress shall make no law respecting the establishment of religion or prohibiting the free exercise thereof." The "Establishment Clause" prohibits the Federal government from establishing a national church or involving itself excessively in religion.

For the most part, this has worked well, but many people today think this means freedom **from** religion in all public areas, including schools, courthouses, parks and other places. This is failure to understand the First Amendment, which was never intended to eliminate God from public life. Constraints have been put on people to the point where they cannot reference faith in any God at any time if done in a public place. This is prohibiting free exercise of religion, and is completely out of place and unconstitutional.

On the other hand, we have a president who is doing his best to introduce the Muslim faith to the American people, which is nothing other than involving himself excessively in religion. If he believed in the Bill of Rights, he could not do this.

Religion has been a part of the warp and woof of American life since the Pilgrims first set foot on our shores, and has been one of the things contributing to our greatness as a nation.. We have been free to orient our lives around what or who we consider to be our God, building lives with confidence on the wisdom we can gain from his direction. This is slowly being eroded as the politicians in Washington have been redirecting people from reliance on themselves and God to reliance on the federal government. Many people like this because reliance on God requires individual responsibility in all of life, but reliance on the "gov'ment" check carries no demands or responsibilities whatsoever. Politicians, by causing this to happen, are helping people lose their sense of need for God.

When people no longer worship God, but commit their lives to the State, deterioration of the quality of life declines for all of us. It is not surprising that morality, the sense of doing what is right, has dramatically declined all over our nation. If we do not reverse our dependence on government and return to dependence on God and ourselves, this will continue to decline. What many people fail to understand is that obeisance to man requires giving up obeisance to anything else, including God.

Many examples of our moral decline could be cited, but only one will be mentioned. Since 1978, 40 million abortions have been performed in the United States. Most people understand that human life is a gift of God, who, allowing us to participate in the act of creation, holds us responsible and accountable to him for what we do with life. We are not responsible to any religion for this belief, but we are responsible directly to God. Being as our legislators have kicked both religion and God out of their deliberations, it is no wonder that so many lives have been destroyed since 1978.

The high school in Alabama scheduled baccalaureate services in the local Baptist church because it was the only facility large enough. Out of the entire community, one person complained. The ACLU jumped in and got the courts to prohibit using the church building. The people defied this and held the program there anyway. Good for them.

When one person or a group of people, including the ACLU and even the courts, trample the rights of people to exercise freedom of assembly, even if it is in a church, they have gone beyond what is right and good in this country. They have gone beyond the provisions of our Constitution and Bill of Rights

A belief in God cannot be proven scientifically, and many people accept only what can be proved this way. To them, provable facts are all that exists. If they cannot get their minds around it and manipulate it, they have no way of understanding that it can exist. They do not understand that some things in life profoundly transcend our level of experience. In so many words, they are saying, "You do me wrong by doing what I don't understand and what I don't want done." The inability to see beyond one's own personal experience is a problem to many people.

For a person to say, "Everyone has to believe and behave as I desire," is nothing less than an effort to take away the freedom people have to build their own lives as desired, and denotes the lack of ability to be comfortable inside one's own skin. If she/he feels the possibility of being contaminated by simply being in a church building, there you have poor strength of character. Many students do not attend baccalaureate services; some of my classmates did not attend the one held in a church when we graduated, but they made no fuss about it. The young person who filed the complaint in Alabama may have desired to attend, but he did not have to do so. Rather, he sought to impose his own way upon his fellow students and the entire community. To seek to control what others do is not a part of the American character.

Some people just don't get what it means to live in a country where it is not permitted for the government or individuals to interfere with freedom of assembly and free exercise of religion, even if they don't believe as others believe. Forcing other people to do things according to your beliefs is clear denial of freedom for others. This was not even a religious service. It was a baccalaureate service that met in the only space large enough to house it. When something like this happens, we can refer to it as tyranny of the few.

Perhaps the ACLU and others of like-mind would like to disprove the existence of love between a man and a woman. It is something you cannot prove scientifically, but you can see signs of it, and, of course, sometimes these signs are misleading..

The America I grew up in opened limitless possibilities for me. I had the promise that, if I did well with the potential God had created within me, I could enjoy the fruits of my labor. Politicians have changed this because they have stepped in and said that reliance on God is not necessary. They have been saying to Americans, "All you need is us. You can give up reliance on God and rely completely on us." Many unthinking people have fallen for this. To replace our religion of reliance on God and ourselves with reliance on politicians will always result in a skewed life for the entire nation. You cannot replace reliance on God with reliance on man and have good results.

The old saying, "Give a man a fish, and you will feed him for a day; teach him how to fish and he will feed himself for a lifetime," is still true. Tragically, the democratic party and a few others have chosen to give people fish today so they will come back to the trough tomorrow. Many of these people lack the ability to understand how dependent they have become on these handouts from Washington or the fact that these handouts have destroyed their ability to earn a living and contribute to the strength of this nation.

We are not a free people when politicians take over the role of being our savior. When they do this, they tax us beyond what is reasonable, and this takes away our freedom in many areas. When the government steps in to be a god for people, all of us lose some amount of freedom because the system politicians set up makes us all serve them in some capacity.

One of the things God asks of us is that we be responsible for who and what we are. When I am forced to pay for the care of people who are just as capable of caring for themselves as I am, I have to help pay for something that allows people to escape their individual responsibility to God. When this happens, it is definitely a religious issue. Paying Caesar to do what people should do for themselves removes the need for them to find their purpose for living as children of God. We all have something to contribute to the world, but we are severely limited when we choose to do the will of government.

Just recently, my wife and I noticed an ad on TV telling people who were receiving government assistance they could get a free phone. "Cast your lot with the government and all your needs will be met." With a message like this growing louder and louder, why should anyone feel a need to rely on themselves and God? And, guess where this money comes from: out of the pockets of taxpayers. Perhaps someone should tell the legislators there are many taxpaying people in this country whose lives are being diminished because they are having to buy things for non-productive people they cannot afford for themselves. Those who cast their lot with government:

1) do not learn to stand on their own two feet, thus avoiding their responsibility to God and themselves, **and** their fellow human beings,

2) lose their sense of the need to develop their talents to serve others, thus seeing little need for education/training,

3) lose confidence in their ability to earn a living. "I have no skills" is what is often heard from the lips of those who have received government assistance over the years.

4). give up plans to attend school and learn a profession for fear they can't make it. Why should they even try when their money arrives in a government envelope each month? People on government assistance have been heard to say, "You people who work are crazy when you can stay home and get money for doing nothing."

5). lose the ability to evaluate and vote for politicians other than the ones who promise them a continuing flow of money. Their ability to be objective is entirely eliminated. The only thing of importance to many of them is, "How much is in it for me?" The welfare of all the people in this country is of little concern to them, only what they think is best for them.

6). lose the ability to be good role models for their children. Because children learn a lot about motivation, the price that must be paid to earn success, their work ethic, the necessity of education, discipline needed in everyday life, and many other things from their parents, millions of children reach adulthood with no hopes of becoming productive citizens. They learn to live off the "gov'ment" because that is what they learned from their parent(s). They have to rely on politicians confiscating money from productive people to give them, and they become comfortable with this. It is no wonder that children born into families dependent on government assistance will themselves be dependent on the government when they become adults.

7). lose the ability to dream big dreams for themselves. Welfare people do not earn Pulitzer prizes or Nobel prizes. They are not on the cutting edge of anything in medicine, technology or anything in the humanities. They do not make contributions to bettering the lives of their neighbors. They do not make the United States a better country for all. They do not do these things because they are waiting on the government check from Washington, which makes no requirement that they do anything of value.

8). do not develop a hunger for achievement. Just as with the lady who said, "Welfare is guaranteed poverty," recipients of government assistance lose that part within that cries out for accomplishment. There is no need to achieve anything when they know the "gov'ment" check will arrive on time.

9). often live in a world devoid of responsibility and replete with abandonment. It is not unusual in my work with clients in classes and individual clinical evaluations to hear such things as, "I never knew my father or mother," or, "My dad left when I was four, and I have never seen him since." One of the huge, complicating things men run up against is the reality that, if they abandon their families, these families will be better off financially because the government will give them more money than they could earn. The "gov'ment" check has made millions of men useless to their families because it has resulted in them abandoning their responsibilities as fathers.

The freedoms we enjoy in America have come through great sacrifice and struggle on the part of many people, and enhancing our freedoms in the future will require struggle. We need all Americans participating in helping correct our weaknesses, making this a stronger nation for those who come after us. Legislators and presidents have tried to eliminate struggle from the lives of people, and this has caused a serious decline in our ability to care for ourselves. Where there is no struggle, we lose strength to live the good life. There is no struggle involved in accepting the "gov'ment" check.

The government has had help taking the life out of people. Not only have individuals abused the original good intentions of programs to help the needy, but groups and organizations have joined the effort to assist people in avoiding their responsibilities to become productive citizens. Among these organizations are many churches who have compiled lists of government programs where people can receive money without having to show a legitimate need for it, and this has been followed by seminars designed to help parishioners find the "free" money. The bottom line of this is churches, in teaching people to abuse a system, are helping them avoid their responsibilities to use their God-given talents and abilities to make this world a better place for everyone.

What a lot of organizations do not realize is that they are not only encouraging, but assisting people in becoming subservient to the masters in Washington, which is the modern-day equivalent of slavery. People lose freedom to build life as they wish it to be built, and become vassals of those who promise them more and more. In order to continue receiving something for nothing, the freedom to vote for the best people is eliminated by the need to vote for those who will promise to take care of them. This is the modern-day form of slavery at its best, and millions of people have chosen to be a part of it. No-one is free when they become dependent on other people taking care of them.

The fully healthy and capable lady who said she was not going to take the job offered her because "it paid only a little more than my welfare check," is a willing victim of a governmental program that damages and destroys the best that is in us. Acceptance of handouts is nothing other than abandonment of one's reason for living. We are made to be more than a sponge, soaking up what is around us. We are made for the purpose of making a contribution to life.

RESPONSIBILITY & STRUGGLING FOR SUCCCESS: NOW BEING DISCOURAGED

All people have concepts about life and how it is to be lived. Some of these concepts are quite simple, having been arrived at with little thought, often handed down from generation to generation, while others have gone to great lengths to study life, what it means and how it is to be lived.

When I and my fellow Americans grew up, we responded positively to what we learned, understanding that our families would not eat unless we worked hard. We were given the choice, one offered to all Americans, to attend school and prepare for whatever occupation we might choose. Many studied and prepared themselves, and were successful. We did what we did based on what we believed about life. A good life was there for the taking, and most of us took it. I never heard anyone suggest that I could sit back, do nothing and have my basic needs met, but many others did. We formed opinions/concepts regarding how we should live life, and most of us have stayed with this all our lives. With few exceptions, we repeated the environment we grew up in. This is why welfare children, when they grow up, become welfare parents.

The story in today's world is different from the way it used to be: you can go home, sit down, and do absolutely nothing. You can be idle, contributing nothing to the well-being of our nation, and, yet, receive your inadequate monthly check from the government in Washington. You do not have to take responsibility for making something of your lives; the politicians will take care of you.

For a long time, the government has paid women to bring more babies into the world, and have excused men from their God-given responsibilities of being dads. With no responsibility to rear children, what did the males do but run around impregnating as many willing females as they wished, feeling no responsibility to do what nature made them to do. This is why the man in class could say he had nine children, all by different women, and did nothing to take care of them; the government would provide money for their care. Another man said he had 13 children by seven different women.

A colleague told about overhearing a conversation his mildly retarded daughter had with a friend, who was also mildly retarded. His daughter, who had one child from a failed marriage, said, "I do not have as much money as I need." Her friend replied, "If you want more money, have another baby. The government will send you another check." The sad thing is that she was telling the absolute truth. Many women in this country are doing this same thing, having babies only because the government will send them more money.

A man at church told about volunteering to work with children in a poor community near Turner Field in Atlanta. He said he loves his work. One day he told us, "100 percent of the children do not live with both parents, and 75 percent live with neither parent." The programs emanating from the government in Washington are responsible for most of this. These children have little chance in life, but what the government is doing is guaranteeing more of this. In the process, they are helping people destroy themselves and the children they bring into the world. For children growing up where parents abandon all parenting responsibilities, and with little to no exposure to responsibility for things they do, it is quite easy for them to run away from their responsibility to care for their own offspring. A sign of maturity is acceptance of responsibility, but our government is encouraging and helping people to avoid the responsibility of parenthood, as well as many other things.

Studies show there is no substitute for parents, and there never has been. Being abandoned by either of the parents is one of the most devastating emotional injuries a child can receive. When both parents abandon, there is double injury. Adoptive parents or childcare organizations can do good work in rearing some of these children, but they will always suffer deficits in life.

The Great Society programs, enacted under President Lyndon Johnson, are great examples of politicians attempting to do for people what they should do for themselves, and the failure which is inherent in such programs.

The **War on Poverty** was a mixture of forty programs which were intended to eliminate poverty by improving living conditions and enabling people to lift themselves out of the cycle of poverty. Of course, millions of people remained in poverty. Lifting people out of poverty is not something the government can do. We have spent billions of dollars in this program, and we still have significant rates of poverty, with the highest level of poverty in 51 years occurring in 2008 (USA Today). The current recession is partly to blame for this, but we should remember the primary cause of the economic disaster we are now in lies with the efforts of legislators in Washington to move poor people out of the slums and ghettos and into middle class and better communities.

Government programs are a guarantee that poverty will always be with us because legislators are doing the wrong things. They are using tax money to remove recipients from their role of being responsible for themselves. Giving people money can change the environments in which they live, but it does not change what is on the inside of them, which is the primary cause of poverty.

Instead of saying to poor people, "We will bail you out," legislators should be saying, "We will assist you as you bail yourself out." This would say to people that self-care is their business, not the business of government. The problem is that legislators will not do this, because it removes people from dependency on them, which, in turn, means loss of votes at the next election.

The Great Society **Education program** was comprised of sixty separate bills that provided for new and better-equipped classrooms, minority scholarships, and low-interest loans. Some of this was good, but the quality of education has declined since then. As an individual who has worked with people with no formal education to those with 20 years beyond high school, this author is appalled at the inability of high school, college, and advanced degree school graduates to handle simple math, science, English, and other things, such as the ability to think and reason about most things in life. Of course, we are all aware that our students have fallen behind students from other nations in many areas.

The public education program in this country has failed our people in the last 60 years. We may find, if we dare compare, that the quality of our educational system took a nosedive with the creation of the Department of Education.

Education became cabinet level in 1979, which meant the legislators placed more emphasis on government doing what citizens should be doing. Although there was great debate regarding whether it was unconstitutional for the federal government to provide education, legislators did it anyway. As in most cases, the government approach has proved inferior to what citizens could have done without interference from Washington.

The Great Society programs of **Medicare and Medicaid** guaranteed healthcare delivery to every American over the age of sixty-five. There have been good things for some people, but, being developed by politicians with little knowledge of healthcare, both programs were so full of holes that costs skyrocketed far beyond what was intended. As an example, in one of the four hospitals where I was CEO, one of the physicians told about admitting an elderly mother to the hospital for two weeks so her daughter and husband could take a vacation to Florida. She was not sick, but Medicare paid the hospital bill plus the physician bill for two visits per day to look after the lady. There was no requirement that a person be sick in order to be admitted to the hospital. Multiply this millions of times, and you have the results of legislators not knowing what they were doing.

In this same hospital, I was able to increase revenue by a multiple of five just by playing by the rules handed me by Medicare and Medicaid legislation. Costs skyrocketed across our nation as hospitals and doctors took advantage of the ineptness of this legislation. I could give chapter and verse of many other situations where government regulations and lack thereof opened the door for significant abuse by individuals and companies. Most healthcare professionals are good, honest people, but the door was wide open for the unscrupulous to line their pockets. This was because the politicians in Washington thought they could solve a problem that was best solved by citizens.

Since the beginnings of Medicare and Medicaid, some problems have been resolved, but they still offer opportunities for healthcare professionals to do things they should not do and get paid for doing these things.

This writer has little confidence that Obama Care will prove to be anything other than a program with holes all in it. The senators and congress men and women who voted for it did not know what was in it, so it will probably be a pig in a poke, and will cost far more than intended. Of course, the politicians plan to take whatever money is needed out of the pockets of productive people to pay for this.

The **Head Start** program was for four-and five-year-old children from disadvantaged families that gave them a chance to start school on an even basis with other children. This program was begun because parents were not doing their jobs as parents. It was a good program in many respects, but it removed from parents one of their primary responsibilities, that of preparing their children for whatever was ahead. What was lacking in this was a program designed to help parents assume the responsibilities inherent in bringing children into the world. It was another case of the government saying to poor people, "If you don't do your job, we'll do it for you," and it sucked more people into dependence on the largess of the federal government.

Children deserve better than what is available in many families. They are gifts to us and need nurturing from the time of birth. Instead of developing programs which let people avoid their jobs, we need to make certain they are going to be required to do for children what children need. Without the background of needed parental care, many of the children who are products of Head Start now reside in jails and prisons. The family is the key to the future success of children, but, unless we develop a society where parents understand this and assume their responsibilities, our jails and institutions will continue to be full of people who should not be there.

If you are seeking to avoid your responsibilities in life, liberal legislators in Washington are waiting with open arms to receive and care for you.

WE NO LONGER FEEL SAFE

Within the past week, my wife and I took target practice with the firearms we recently purchased. We were reluctant to purchase handguns, but the reality of what is happening in our communities left us with little choice. Some people claim the ownership of guns does not improve safety, but gun ownership in other nations tells a different storey - or in Kennesaw, Georgia, where crime plummeted when an ordinance requiring each home to own a firearm became law.

The feeling of safety we had when I was growing up is only a memory. There are now very few places where, if alone, I feel completely safe. Under no circumstances do I feel completely safe anywhere in Atlanta if I am alone, whether this be during the daytime or at night. I have gotten to the place where

I will not go to Atlanta in early evening or at night, and I always feel uneasy when my wife goes for medical appointments in one of the best areas in Atlanta.

In the late 1970's we moved into a middle class suburb of Atlanta. For many years, safety in our community and city was a given, with us never having a concern about it. Then the community started changing as people on government assistance programs, i.e. welfare, food stamps, "liar loans" from Freddie Mac and Fannie Mae they had no hope of repaying, began moving into the community. About four years ago my wife finally talked me into locking my car doors when I went somewhere for fear of carjacking - even in our previously great community. About that same time, because she had a habit of walking in the neighborhood, I purchased a stun gun for protection in the event she was attacked. Then, recently we added the personal handguns.

In the last six to eight years, crime has skyrocketed in about all areas where statistics are kept. We now see drug dealings in front yards near where we live; robberies have dramatically increased; carjackings have moved out of Atlanta into our county; murders have dramatically increased, nine narcotics agents with drawn weapons surrounding a house in my neighborhood, etc., etc.

My wife and I do not like the feeling of being unsafe. Neighbors we know and people at church tell us they feel the same way we do. At the present time, we have little hope there will ever be a time in our community when we can again feel safe. With politicians continuing to develop programs which encourage idleness and dependence on the "gov'ment" check, our sense of insecurity will increase as people are led to believe it is okay to live off the success of other people. The message coming out of Washington for several years is that poor people are entitled to take from others what does not belong to them. Thus, we are seeing individuals and gangs going into stores and taking what they desire without paying for it.

In many other areas of life, our safety has diminished. The June, 2011 issue of Consumer Reports lists 25 things we need to do to protect ourselves from crooks. There were suggestions on how to protect your home, your financial records, your computer, your car, your credit cards, your medical records and prescriptions. It seems there are crooks everywhere just looking for ways to take things from you. The society I grew up in could never have dreamed there would be no place, whatsoever, where a person could feel safe. In a brief conversation about this recently, my wife said, "We have more sorry people than we used to have." She was exactly correct. I cannot think of a place I could feel 100 percent safe, and that includes my church.

Of course, much of this has been created by our politicians in Washington.

CHAPTER THREE

THE SOURCE OF OUR DECLINE

When we look for the source of our decline, signs are everywhere. There is no institution free of signs of decay, from the lowliest of people whose morals allow them to take what does not belong to them, to clerics who consider sexual abuse of others to be okay, to politicians whose attempts to be savior to people makes them worthless. A few of the reasons for our decline will be mentioned.

POLITICIANS ARE DESTROYING AMERICA

When looking at the history of the United States, we can point our fingers at many things we have not done right, from slavery to the fat cats on Wall Street to failure to prepare for those nations who would destroy us, i.e., Germany and Japan to the criminals who take what does not belong to them, and to many other things. But, we have survived them all. We've done so because we have been a strong, free nation with a free market system giving honor to our dependence on a power greater than ourselves. There is no nation which has been able to pose a threat to our security.

But, now we face the greatest threat to our security and continuance as a free nation we have ever faced, and the threat is not coming from outside our borders. It has come and is coming from the politicians in Washington. What they are doing is destroying the best nation this world has ever known.

Why are they doing this? There can be only one of two reasons. First, they are destroying this nation because they do not understand what they are doing. We can probably rule this out because a limited intelligence quickly reveals that spending more money than you take in is a road to disaster, as is paying people not to work, making them dependent on the handout of money confiscated from taxpayers.

The second reason is **they know what they are doing and it is their intention to destroy us.** If our president and Congress had intended to strengthen our nation, they would not have deliberately done so much to hurt us, and done it in a way that betrayed the American way of life They would not have surrounded themselves with communists, socialists and extreme liberals, and they would not have engaged in the deceit, lies, bribery, and disregard of the American people which has been characteristic since the last election. They have known what they have been doing, and they have escalated actions as their terms of office have progressed.

Why would they do this? First, the liberal politicians under the dome have placed their welfare ahead of the welfare of the entire nation. They know that, if they take money from productive people and give it to poor, lazy people who choose not to work that these people will vote for them, returning them to office to do more of the same. This is a despicable way to treat both the taxpayers and the poor people because it removes from taxpayers what rightly belongs to them and it undermines the ability of poor people to stand on their own feet.

Second, there are some people in Washington who wish to be in charge of everything that happens, and, if there is enough collapse of our economy, that could happen. A person could step forward and proclaim, "I am the one who can rescue you," and many Americans would give him/her anything desired. Some people say this could never happen in the United States, but the pages of history are full of examples of this very same thing happening. One of the latest of these took place during the last century as the most intelligent nation in the world democratically elected a leader who then eliminated democracy and cancelled elections. He wanted to be king of the world, and the result was the death of 60 million people.

Some people would claim such talk as this is generating great fear. No, it is not. It is suggesting the need for us to engage our minds and learn from history, becoming aware that no nation is beyond becoming mesmerized by a person or persons claiming to be our savior(s).

We have recently been experiencing new rules, regulations and laws coming from the Oval Office and Congress that are totally alien to us having a representative government. Things the American people have not wanted have been shoved down our throats, and it has taken us a long way toward being a nation never intended by the Founding Fathers.

Many writers have tried to be diplomatic regarding what is going on in Washington, but the time has arrived where we must understand that the verbiage coming from the lips of politicians has not agreed with what they have done.

Yes, our nation is being destroyed by the politicians in Washington.

POLITICIANS HAVE KICKED GOD OUT

It is no wonder things have become such a mess in Washington. It could not be otherwise because for years legislators have ignored their own frailty and limitations, paying little attention to the real source of what is best for all Americans. They have limited themselves to what the human mind can see. In doing so, they have set themselves up as the final arbiters of all things. They have, in other words, kicked God out of their lives and are left with no sense of their need for a wisdom beyond their own.

It is okay to kick religion out of politics, but not God. Religion is the product of man's mind, as is indicated by the requirement that, to be a part of a religion, you have to accept a body of beliefs and practices. One must say, "I believe what you tell me to believe." Add to this the requirement that you practice religion in a certain way, and you have religions seeking to control every aspect of a person's life. If you do not adhere to the guidance of religion, you become unacceptable, and lose freedom to build your own life as you see fit. In some religions, you may be killed for not following the dictates of dogma and the clerics

Not so with God. God extends to each of us complete freedom to make our way in life. We can choose to follow the wisdom which has its source in him or we can choose to go our own way. Whichever we choose, we remain completely acceptable to him. His love for us is diminished in no way by how we respond to him, and he still makes his wisdom available if we are interested.

When politicians and others confuse religion with God, kicking both out of their lives, they limit themselves to the machinations of their own minds. We are not only told this by the folly of men throughout history, but we are confronted on a daily basis with the results of basing lives on human wisdom.

Politicians have lost their sense of responsibility to the American people. This always leads to the kind of discriminatory decisions we have seen coming from Capitol Hill. When people are in touch with God, they understand that the process of hurting one group of people in order to help another group is not acceptable. A hallmark of man's wisdom is disregard of the need for fairness in the things we do. This has been easy to see in Washington for a long time, but it has leaped out at us more powerfully than ever during the last three years.

Kicking religion out of deliberations is okay, but, when there is little to no recognition of the existence of God, we might be tempted to conclude of this administration and Congress that they are a bunch of godless people doing things which have little resemblance to what is best for our country. When people associate themselves with God, it shows, and when they do not, it shows. The deceit, lying, bribery, discrimination and misuse of many things these past three years is good indication of the absence of anything to do with God.

Many of the people in Congress are religious and attend church on a regular basis. However, sometimes attending church means little. This author has been in church all his life, and has concluded that some of the meanest people he has ever known have been active church members. In order to effectively lead people and do what is best for them, it takes more than merely claiming to be God-fearing. God is not the author of bringing hurt into the lives of people, but we see this happening again and again in Washington.

If presidents and legislators could recognize their responsibility to God and their fellow Americans, they could not lie about what they are doing, they could not make exclusive deals with certain groups at the expense of others, they could not bribe to get their way, they could not develop systems which trap good people in welfare, they could not pass legislation without reading it, and they could not do many other things which betray the freedoms upon which this nation was founded. Leadership without awareness of the need to see truth beyond what the human eye can see will always bring the kind of national troubles we have been experiencing for many years. Kicking God out of the halls of Congress has never been a good idea and it never will be.

Since the beginnings of recorded history, and no doubt before, most people have felt something well up from deep within pointing toward a Power greater than themselves. We have made attempts to give this Power a name, and we have come up with such names as Buddha, Allah, Jehovah, Deus, Ishvara, Vishnu, Achaman, The Great Spirit, Yahweh,, God and others, but we are all referring to this same Power. Our religious problems/differences have come when we have sought to arrive at a definition/description of who and what this Power is, and most of us think we have figured him out. A great difficulty we have in this is that we are stuck with human wisdom attempting to understand something which cannot be understood. But, non-the less, we persist, and form our concepts, dogma, statements of faith, etc., on intellectual determination of this power. Of course, when we do this, we develop different beliefs because our understandings boil down to our own ideas.

We use these differences centered in our mind to put down and discriminate against those who do not determine this Power to be what we have determined him to be, and we develop feelings of superiority because "we have gotten it right." This allows us to force our religious beliefs on other people. This is the problem with religion and government being in bed together.

Probably no religion has gotten everything right about this Power, and we need to cease thinking we have. We need to come to an understanding that we do not find God (the name with which this writer is most familiar), by going to the mind of other men. We find him as we make contact with him on an individual basis, basically in response to his initiative to love us. He touches us and we respond.

Our legislators need to understand that, by kicking God out with religion, they are left without the wisdom they need to do their work, and have great difficulty determining the right things to do.

With the definition, "God is love," which comes from the Holy Bible (I John 4:16), with which I am familiar, we have what should be the basis of how we treat each other. This is what is sorely missing on Capitol Hill, the Oval Office, and much of the life of citizens across our nation. Kicking religion out is okay, but kicking God out leaves us with dependence on our discriminatory, human wisdom.

This writer has yet to be exposed to a religion that opens its doors and says, "Y'all come and let's learn how to be brothers." The Great Crusades and the shout, "Kill the satanic Americans," remind us of what is generated by the human mind under the control of religion rather than the freedom found in God. God, who is love, will never hurt us in any way, but man will when he views other humans through the lenses of religion.

The mind influenced by God is an entirely different matter, for to be moved with the touch of God is to have our wills channeled toward things which draw people together. With God there is no room for brother to be set against brother, and we come to see differences as opportunities to learn and grow, not opportunities to take up arms against each other. "Our way or the highway," a message that pervades many religions and most governments, is good indication of the absence of God.

Those politicians in Washington who operate without the wisdom of God have no possibility of seeing what cannot be seen with the human mind. When left to our own connivings, we will do our best to stack life in our favor regardless of what happens to our neighbor. When we are in contact with God, our minds begin to understand something of the dignity of human beings, and the need we have to treat each other with utmost respect.

When our founders recognized God in the establishment of this nation, it was rather astounding. They gave us all the beginnings of freedom and recognized this as a gift of God. To turn our backs on this, which is what many in Washington have done and want to do, is a guarantee of retreat into a nation run without the wisdom of God. This can never give us the quality of a nation under God.

Our march toward recognizing that "all men are created equal," and "are endowed by their Creator with certain unalienable Rights, and that among them are Life, Liberty and pursuit of Happiness" is a march that has been, at best, uneven, and will never end if we remain a Constitutional Republic. It is a march much slower than desired, but it is certain if we stay in touch with the wisdom that comes from above. Some of the drafters of our Constitution and Bill of Rights had difficulty understanding some of what they had done. Both George Washington and Tomas Jefferson had slaves. Had they understood what they had written, they could not have owned human beings. **It takes time for people to learn to do right.** One of the great things about our founding documents is that they, for the first time in history, laid the foundation for people to be free. Some would say this is a gift of God that transcends the wisdom of man.

What we have glaringly seen during these past three years is a setback to freedom and equality for all. The streams of lies, behind closed doors deal-making, discrimination one entity against the other, bribery given and received in order to pass legislation, the extraction of far more money from citizen's pockets than can be justified to give to people who have chosen idleness to production, the attempt to force many unwanted things down the throats of Americans, escalation of class warfare like we have never before experienced, efforts against our wishes to replace constitutional government with socialism, and other things which have already diminished quality of life for a majority of our citizens are not in keeping with a nation slowly, but surely, moving toward equality for all. Much of what has come out of the minds of the politicians in Washington these last three years is irrational and has greatly interfered with a better life being offered to all our people. It has created divisions among us far greater than we have seen in the past 60 years.

History has shown us that the march toward freeing mankind from his self-imposed shackles is a slow one, but that, in this country, we have made far more progress than any other nation.

POLITICAL FOUNDATION OF DECISION-MAKING

"Life should be lived as we determine" is the constant message coming out of legislation passed by the politicians in Washington. What has become clear to this writer over a period of years is that my rights to be who and what I want to be have been greatly diminished by politicians who think they know what is best for me. This has reached a crescendo in the last three years as the democrats interpreted control of Congress as giving them carte blanche to impose their ways upon me and all my fellow citizens. They want my future and that of everyone to be based on what they think is best for us. They wish to limit my freedom to use my resources to build the kind of life I desire, and depend on their benevolence (with taxpayer's money) to do what they think is best. This is taking us rapidly toward a disaster, and we are already seeing signs of the collapse of our nation.

A good example of this is Obama Care. Americans overwhelmingly objected to it, but the democrats passed it by telling lie after lie, by discriminating against certain states and segments of our population, by intimidation, by back-room deals, by out and out bribery, and by passing a huge bill without even so much as reading it. The bill could not stand on its own merits, but Obama and the democrats found a way to shove it down our throats by bribing people and organizations to get their support. If the leaders of private industry were to do something like this, the politicians in Washington would find a way to throw them all in jail.

The strength of our nation does not lie in the elected officials we send to Washington. It resides in the American people. The wisdom of the people is far superior to the wisdom under the dome, but politicians do not believe this as they desire to think of themselves as the crème de la crème of our nation. They have been given the votes of the people, but this did not convey upon them a special dispensation of knowledge and wisdom. They have forgotten they are servants of all the people, and not just a minority whose votes they can buy with their give-away programs.

Many poor people in this country seem to relish control of their lives being in the hands of politicians. It removes from them the task of providing for themselves, and being responsible to God for what they do; they can just sit back and wait on the money from Washington. It also removes them from being constructive contributors to improving the freedoms we have. Politicians do not want freedom for citizens, which comes with God in our lives; what they want are people who will buy into the idea that they cannot make it in this life without gifts from Washington.

For productive people, control from Washington is severe limitation of what individuals can accomplish when living in an environment which rewards rather than punishes them for being successful. Productive people are responsible in that they see their future being in their own hands, and realize the only source of the good life lies in what they are able to produce with the talents and abilities they have. The tax dollars taken from productive people limits what they can accomplish because money taken from their pockets could be used to help them be more successful, providing more jobs for more people.

Government does far less with money than productive citizens. Politicians wrangle over legislation and develop programs which are always flawed, leaving room for great waste of money. Ask a productive person to build a program, and that person will build it well and it will be done less expensively than if done by government. Give the same job to the government, and it might turn out to be half as good, take longer to build, and probably cost at least twice as much. Many things in life could be better if the government kept its hands off.

WE THE PEOPLE, though often far from what we ought to be, do recognize that we are a nation under God and must remain so if we are to continue our quest to find true freedom for all our people. Political wisdom is a poor substitute for the wisdom we need to make this an even more successful nation than it has ever been. The results of political wisdom over the past 80 years are easily seen in the deterioration it has brought us in the many laws emanating from Washington, programs which have progressively removed from the American people their right to live free from governmental constraints. More and more of our freedoms will be removed if legislators continue their failure to listen to productive people, and to give recognition to their responsibility under God to build a nation of fairness to all.

ABANDONMENT OF CONSTITUTIONAL GOVERNMENT

It is quite clear, and has been for a long time, that the politicians we have sent to Washington have not believed in the Constitution of the United States. If they did believe in it, they could not have done some of the things they have done. This is particularly personified in our current president and many with whom he has surrounded himself as they are doing their best to install a socialist form of government, one in which people become subservient to the power structure in Washington. They have been and are doing this because they do not understand the Constitution and Bill of Rights, the two founding documents that have led us to become the greatest nation the world has ever seen. It is further quite clear that Mr. Obama wants government to be based on what comes out of his mind. Laws seem to mean very little to him; he feels he has license to do whatever he wants to do. To him, what is legal is what he wants.

This greatness of our nation does not spring from what happens under the dome in Washington when men and women deliberate and pass laws, no matter who these people might be. No one person or group of persons has any possibility of knowing what is best for me and my fellow Americans. That is our decision to make. A socialist form of government requires me to orient my life around what humans expect and demand of me, and this is perhaps the shakiest way there is for me to run my life. Given freedom to build my life the way I want to build it opens up the opportunity to consider the source and purpose of my life. When I begin to deal with this, rather than with the expectations and demands of elected officials, I begin to get in touch with something man cannot give me. That something is the source and purpose of my life, and, when I begin to consider this, my life takes on new meaning because I am then introduced to my Creator and the responsibility I have as one made in his image.

The great failures in human history can be traced to the inability of people to recognize their responsibilities to each other as people made in the image of God. Much of mankind is out of touch with the source of that which makes life good, and, when we do not have this connection, we are limited to what human wisdom can give us. This is never adequate for the needs we face day in and day out.

GOVERNMENTAL ABUSE OF POOR PEOPLE

Our federal government has probably done more harm to poor people than all other organizations combined. This is a strong statement, but allow me to explain. One of the most devastating things that can be done to an individual is to take away his/her opportunities to achieve a flourishing life. When we come into this world, we are all equipped to succeed at something if given the proper environment, challenge and encouragement.

Liberal politicians have developed a multitude of what is called "entitlement programs," and they have sucked millions of people into believing they are entitled to a lot of stuff simply because they exist. They do not have to do anything to earn their way.

When considering the nature of human beings, it is good to ask if we were designed to achieve a good life. Does each of us have a purpose or were we all accidents with no meaning? Are we things to be used by others or do we have the capacity to build good lives for ourselves? Are individuals created to be something or do something or are we pawns in the hands of others? These questions scare liberals/socialists because they imply an intent above and beyond the mind of man. For the socialist, people are to be controlled, to be what they are told to be, do what they are told to do when they are told to do it the way they are told to do it. People are not to stand on their own two feet, but depend on others for all their needs.

Entitlement programs kill the life within people. When we are made to accomplish things in our lives, but live with the absence of purpose, we cannot find that for which we were made. The life that is best lived is the one where the individual takes his/her potential, develops it and achieves a worthy goal. When we come to a realization of this, we become aware of our individual uniqueness, something that is repeated nowhere else in the world. To understand this is to understand that no-one else can make the contribution we individually can make.

Unproductive people can develop the ability to take care of themselves if the government gets out of their way. This was abundantly clear prior to the Great Society Program and the welfare state that followed. If a healthy man does not have a piece of bread to eat, he will go find it, most of the time by working so he can buy it. Entitlement programs tell people they have to do nothing in order to eat and enjoy other things in life, and so millions sit down, do nothing and wait on a handout of money from Washington, money which has been taken away from those who do work. When the next month arrives, they again do nothing and wait on the largess from government, etc., etc.

If we do not pursue becoming who we were made to be, developing and using our talents for something worthwhile, but spend our time waiting for others to take care of us, we lose our talents and become totally dependent on others for our daily care. This is called dependency, and it robs people of the best life can offer.

A serious problem many Americans face is absence of an environment in which they are challenged to be who they were made to be. When entitlements become a way of life, there is no need to concern ourselves with doing good or amounting to anything. But, to turn our lives over to others is a certain way of losing our individual opportunities to build a flourishing life, which comes only through living life as we want to live it.

It is estimated that, when we are born, we have approximately 100 billion brain cells. Every person has these if they are born free of disease or injury. This suggests that, in the beginning, we are all on a level playing field, with each having the potential to succeed at something. Then the trouble begins. Some of us are born into environments which challenge us to develop the best that is within, learning that life is what we make of it, and we buckle down, study and work hard so we can earn our way. We learn to stand on our own two feet. Others, however, are born into environments offering little to no challenge regarding what life is all about and how they can become successful. They do not see the importance of studying and working hard to make something of themselves. They learn rather quickly they can get by in life with entitlements, where they are required to do nothing.

Learning from their parents and acquaintances that the monthly check will be in the mailbox deprives them of any interest in doing something that is productive and worthwhile. They do not learn to stand on their own two feet because no-one around them has learned to stand on their own two feet. This is where entitlement programs have done so much damage.

One of the things we have all heard for a long time is that, if you do not use something, i.e. a muscle, you will lose it. This applies to the mind as well. If we do not use it, those 100 billion brain cells we receive at birth will waste away, and we will lose whatever potential we brought into the world. Not being required to use our minds is a sure way to have them atrophy over time. Receipt of entitlements idles the brain and guarantees loss of the potential with which we were born.

There is no incentive to work for a paycheck when all we have to do is reach in the mailbox for the "gov"ment" check. A colleague of mine told about a domestic violence class his wife facilitates, and the approach of the welfare recipients in that class, which is as follows, "You are crazy for working when the government will give you money," and they then proceeded to name the various programs from which they can receive money.

The Georgia legislature recently passed a tough immigration law. Many farmers are concerned that illegal aliens will go back home, and they will be stuck with crops rotting in the fields. In seeking to find laborers, one farmer went to an unemployment office where he found several Americans applying for unemployment benefits. Here is what he heard from these unemployed men: "I don't want to work that hard;" "I am not going to work for that amount of money when I can draw unemployment;" "That is too hard for me; I don't think I can do it." These men are wimps, some of them being unable to do manual labor because they have never had to do it, and others just choosing to be lazy. They have no earthly idea what life is all about.

Governor Nathan Deal, Georgia, suggested the use of people on probation to gather crops. A group of them was taken to gather cucumbers. All the probationers quit because it "was too hot." Physically, we cannot compete with people from other cultures.

Entitlement programs have created this mess. If our nation is to survive as a good and great nation, we have no choice but to dramatically change the way our government is making worthless people out of good people. The liberals in Congress, primarily the democrats, must face the fact that they have led in development of welfare programs that have taken the life out of people.

When members of my generation were offered a job, we jumped at the chance to work regardless of what it was if it was an honest job.. That's why this author took his first public job in South Georgia making 50 cents per day (yes, that's fifty cents per day, not per hour). We had pride in ourselves and we were strong enough to tackle any job presented to us. Because of determination and drive like this, we built the greatest economy and nation ever to appear on the face of the earth.

Telling people they do not have to work in order to eat is a sure way to destroy individual lives, but, also, is a sure way of destroying the life of our nation. Tell people without pride in themselves they do not have to work and they won't, and they will cast their lot with those who promise the most. This is the primary reason unproductive people almost always vote for the democrats.

What is wrong with the picture of life being painted in Congress and the White House? Just about everything. We are a far weaker nation now than we were 60 years ago, with much of our deterioration having come directly at the hands of our lawmakers in Washington. There is no way we can remain a strong nation with what they have done to us. The sad thing in this is any halfway intelligent person can easily understand that giving people money for doing nothing eliminates them from productivity and destroys their value to our way of life.

The Washington power structure presents themselves as fairly intelligent, so the question we need to ask is, "Why, if they are intelligent, do they keep doing the things which are destroying us?" If they are indeed intelligent, they must have a purpose in making people useless and dependent on government handouts.

When the government and other organizations identify the poor as incapable of earning their way in this world, they are basically communicating to them that they are inferior. If a person with a lot of initiative were told this, he/she would set about to prove this to be wrong. But, the unproductive poor have accepted this when they curtail efforts to make something of themselves and accept government's largess (largess is what is given to inferior people).

Healthy people have a way of pulling themselves up out of poverty. In a society where people are given access to education and freedom to pursue their dreams, as is true in the United States, those who have a good mind and a good body cannot blame their situation in life on anybody but themselves. **Whatever situation you find yourself in, it is about you, no-one else.** People may have presented you with difficult circumstances, but you have always had the choice to change who you are with, what you are doing, and where you will do it. In my work with clients, some of them have had to move out of state to change their destructive environments, and their lives have dramatically changed for the better because of their courage to do what is in their best interest. A question that is appropriate for every person living on the government dole to ask is, "What is there about me that has led me to choose to be a welfare/entitlement recipient?"

Politicians will keep unproductive poor people poor as long as these people let them. What many poor people do not understand is that money taken from taxpayers can never be enough to give them anything equal to what they can give themselves if they develop their talents and go after life with passion and determination. What politicians give people is a weak mess of pottage compared to what they can give themselves. It is only through determination and effort that they can give themselves the best that life can offer.

One of the areas to which our nation needs to give attention is what I call "people-building." This would involve the process of identifying each person born as a gift to our nation and world, as someone who is valuable beyond our imagination, and worthy of being provided an environment in which they are introduced to opportunities to develop their talents and make something of themselves. Most of the work we do for people is after their lives have fallen apart. We try to help them pick up the pieces and move into the future. We do very little as a nation to help people learn to take care of themselves from the beginning of life. This is where we have unlimited opportunities to help make life better for individuals, families and our nation. We need better people in this world, but much of what we do encourages them to do things which are harmful to themselves and to relationships. A world of employment would be available if we could arrive at an understanding that people-building is one of the most important, if not **the most important**, jobs we could have. Of course, politicians will resist people-building because, were this to take place, people would learn to take care of themselves and would have no need for political handouts.

It is sad to say that unproductive poor people generally lack the ability to understand what our government has done to them. They have been led to believe the government will take care of them, but the monthly check never seems to be enough. The flow of money into their hands has not been adequate to give them what they consider to be the good life. They fail to grasp the fact that the good life cannot be given to a person; it can come only through achievement by that person. A good, rewarding life is what a person gives himself/herself. Rather than doing unproductive poor people a favor by placing unearned money in their hands, the government has actually been responsible for taking the good life away from them.

Being true to ourselves and connecting with our purpose and passion, that which springs from deep within, is where true happiness and fulfillment come from. When people are not true to themselves, allowing other people or organizations to determine what life should be, they lose themselves, and many times reach the point where the richness that was within when they were born cannot be retrieved. This is when people become spiritually and morally empty and depressed as the life meant for them slowly ebbs away. Being without purpose and passion makes individuals vulnerable to those who are all too ready and eager to impose their way of life upon them.

GOVERNMENT ASSISTANCE PROGRAMS: A FORM OF SLAVERY

There is something within each of us that cries out for expression, and, if we do not find a way to express it, life becomes less meaningful and happy than it should be. Sometimes we end up being miserable because we have not found our passion for living.

Caroline came for counseling at age 51 seeking relief from a life of misery. In the first three sessions, she, with tears and great emotion, recounted the misery of her four marriages and the difficulty of finding meaning in her life. She graduated from college and taught school for a number of years, but this proved to be unrewarding. She then opened her own business, and was successful financially, but joy and happiness eluded her. She decided to travel, but this, too, did not bring what she was looking for. At the encouragement of her third husband, she went back to school and received a degree in accounting, but this still was not satisfying. She spoke at length of the miserable relationship she had with her three children, one of whom asked her not to come to his wedding.

Caroline was indeed a miserable person in need of getting in touch with her purpose for living. During the fourth session, the counselor asked the miracle question: "If all your problems could disappear tonight, and you could do anything tomorrow your heart desired, what would that be?" Without a moments hesitation, she blurted out, "I'd be a concert pianist!!!" This was her first mention of music.

The counselor asked if she would like to tell him about that. Her words went like this: "I began to take piano lessons when I was five years old, and I just loved it. Sometimes I practiced so much that my mother would have to threaten me to get me to go to bed. This became my life. I was a good student, so there was time for me to practice. As a teenager, I played at church and for weddings. I was good, and dreamed about going to college to study for a career as a concert pianist.

"My dad had other ideas for me. He was a well-to-do industrialist, made lots of money, and could have sent me to any college to study anything. When I began to tell him about my desire to become a concert pianist, he said that I could not make a living as a musician and that he would not pay my expenses to college if that is what I decided to do. He did not relent, so what was I to do? He said I could make a living as a teacher and he would pay my college expenses if I would become a teacher. I could have run away from home, but then I would have nothing. So, I went to college and became a teacher, but I was terribly unhappy. Then I tried business and travel and then accounting, but I was miserable everywhere. And the relationships with my children brought even more misery as well as my four marriages."

The counselor asked, "Would you still like to study music?" Caroline shot back, "Yes, yes!!!" She acknowledged that it was too late for her to become a concert pianist, but would like to return to college to study piano. She chose a college and completed a degree in piano, and, after graduation, became an adjunct professor of piano at this college. Caroline found her joy, but it was tempered by the limitations which had been placed on her by her dad.

Many of us go through life with family, friends, and the environment telling us they know what is best for us. If we do not reason and think about this, it is easy to accept what they say as the final word, and we miss the fact that our best life comes from developing what is deep within us. We have the power to decide what our life will be, but many people never learn this. We can take control of our lives, and, through choice, rise above the limitations people would place on us. Like Caroline, giving someone else the final word about our lives leads to abandonment of our passion for living, which often leads to misery. Even though she had enough money to have a good life, she was miserable.

When the government says they will take care of us, many feel there is no need to find our passion. By accepting this, the best life possible eludes us. We wind up with a mess of pottage when we could have caviar and steak. We can certainly say, "Welfare brings diminished human value," and this has a great bearing on the joy we can get out of life.

Suspension of one's reasoning and thinking powers is a prerequisite for accepting "free" money from the government. To do your own thinking would lead you to the conclusion that only you can satisfy the longings of your heart.

Depending on others for our care will eventually cause us to ask, "Who will give us the most?" Once we begin to travel this road, we become easy prey to the politician who promises us the most. We can easily get to the place where we have no choice but to vote for the politicians we think are best able to keep taxpayer money flowing into our hands, and thereby we lose our zest for making something out of ourselves.

A friend, having family in Europe, has visited several socialist countries a number of times. Recently returning and talking about her trip, she said, "People in Europe don't smile very much, nothing like they smile here." This is a good commentary on one of the differences found in a country like America where people can pursue their passion, making their own way rather than depending on government to give them their basic needs. We can run our own lives and receive the joy which comes from doing so.

When we begin to think government should determine our lives, we need to think about the old Soviet Union, what has happened to Greece, and what is going on in Portugal. Socialism, in spite of its promises, is never the final word in lifting people to a good life. What we have in America is far superior to anything possible under socialism.

One individual (don't remember who), said, "The soul gives us the ability to think." We all have soul, but we don't all think. It is in our capacity to use what the soul gives us, but many do not do this, preferring to let others do our thinking for us.

The lady (referenced earlier) who said, "Welfare is guaranteed poverty," was the product of an environment in which neither education nor working to earn one's way was emphasized or encouraged. She was surrounded by unproductive non-achievers who were comfortable riding the backs of productive people. She learned it was okay for someone else to take care of her, and, therefore, abandoned all efforts to become a productive member of society. Having concepts like this, there was only one thing that could happen, and that was to accept the largess of those willing to buy her vote.

This lady has become a willing victim of the abuse the government has dumped on poor people. They have been led to abandon their God-given thrust to make something of their lives, and have been relegated to placing their lives in the hands of those who wish to determine what their lives will be. And, so long as people turn down the opportunity to care for themselves, they have no option but to support politicians who promise to continue funneling into their pockets money which has been taken from those who have earned it. **This is nothing other than a form of slavery.** It is not the evil physical slavery we had in the early years of our nation, but it is slavery none-the-less. It is slavery of the mind and spirit. When freedom to build one's life as desired is taken away by any people or program, one is kept in confinement and, therein, you have slavery. Welfare is confinement to a way of life which is limited by the size of the monthly check politicians send them, unless, of course, they resort to crime. Poor people are trapped in this confinement, and, finding themselves without a background in which they have learned to stand on their own two feet, they are boxed in to accepting what other people can give them. They have chosen to permit politicians to rob them of their initiative and effort to build life according to what is on the inside of them. This is gross abuse on the part of the politicians in Washington.

Both poor people and politicians would do well to consider the words of Epictetus, a man who lived 55-135 AD. Born into slavery, he was terribly mistreated, with his master once breaking one of his legs. This master, however, did allow him to receive an education. Later, Epictetus gained freedom and became a well-known and well-respected sage and philosopher. In later years, reflecting on his life, he wrote, "No man is free who is not master of himself." For the government to willingly trap people in lives of dependence, and for individuals to choose to be so trapped is a sure sign of the lack of freedom, which is a form of slavery..

Every person needs the communication, "At'a boy; you can do it!" The message coming out of Washington to poor people, however, is, "You can't do it; you can't make it without the government giving you money."

Politicians who believe it is their duty to take from the rich and give to the poor have had a lot of help from people and organizations who do not understand what God has placed on the inside of each of us. If we could see people as pre-positioned to succeed in life when they are born, we would approach them in an entirely different way from the way we do now. We would see them as full of potential, and that our responsibility is to encourage and assist them in stretching their bodies, minds and spirits to achieve the best they can get from life. It is only when people gird up themselves and pursue life with a passion that the best in life can be theirs. The liberals in Washington do not want people to do this because it would destroy their base of votes. People have no need of politicians and the largess of government when they learn to take care of themselves by becoming achievers with no need of government.

As mentioned earlier, robbing people of their responsibility to make positive contributions to life has also come from churches which have sponsored seminars to help people learn about "free" government money and how to get it. This is a poor way for churches to approach those who are made in the image of God. It is also a powerful communication that the leaders of churches do not believe their people are capable of taking care of themselves. This is not the business churches should be in. Rather, they should be helping people prepare from the beginning of life to build good, productive, satisfying lives built on the talents and abilities they have.

Also helping to rob the poor of their responsibility to achieve in this world are people like Jesse Jackson, Al Sharpton and many others. They have indeed done some good, needed work, and this should be recognized and appreciated, but they have joined the chorus singing, "Poor people are not able to succeed in this life without government money." This kind of thing has been devastating to poor people because it has helped convince them they cannot make it without assistance from Washington. If these people, along with churches and politicians, had spent time working to help poor people learn to stand own their own feet, there would have been millions more with jobs making a positive contribution to life. They would not now be on the government dole, and our nation would never have experienced the entitlement/welfare mess we are in.

People are worth too much to be treated as if they do not have what it takes to care for themselves. To be told from the very beginning that one is inferior and incapable of building a good life is to be dealt a psychological blow from which many people never recover. Epictetus once said, "God has entrusted me with myself." (Information re Epictetus taken from Wikipedia.)

The 30 year old counselee, trying to find out why he lost job after job because of mistakes he made, said, "Can't you see that I am stupid and can't do anything right?" The counselor asked where he had learned he was stupid. He said, "That's what my dad used to tell me all the time when I was growing up." Whenever he would start to do something, it was as if a tape began playing in his head, shouting out the words of his dad, "You are stupid and can't do anything right." In like manner, if you tell poor people often enough they cannot care for themselves, they will grow up believing exactly that. Our federal government has mastered the art of telling poor people they are incapable of self care, and this has led to millions of people being victims of the "Massah" in Washington.

One of the arguments used in the 19th century by some slave owners to help them hold onto their slaves was that slaves did not have the ability to take care of themselves. Some slave owners truly believed this, and so did some of the slaves, who chose to remain with their masters. Many politicians in today's world persist in negating poor people's ability to learn, work and provide for themselves and their families because they want to keep them dependent on handouts from the government, thus guaranteeing votes. This denotes a lack of appreciation for the dignity and worth of individual human beings, and is terrible abuse of people made in the image of God. We need to understand that God makes no junk; it is people who produce the waste of human life. We need to be in the business of people-making instead of people-negating.

Some people may wish to make a race issue out of this, but it is not. Of all the millions now on welfare, 38+ percent are white and 37+ percent are black. The problem is not race, but the culture/environment out of which people come, the welfare program, some churches and other organizations that are designed to perpetuate the culture in which poor people grow up. Welfare and other government programs fail to provide necessary incentives and motivation for poor people to escape their environments.

For everyone who believes some people are unable to care for themselves, we need to remind them of the Tuskegee Airmen, who were told by many from the beginning that they could not become good pilots. They refused to accept this as the final word. They worked hard and became some of the best pilots of the Second World War, having never lost a bomber they escorted. We could point to Dr. Ben Carson, who came out of a welfare environment where he was considered the dumbest kid in his fifth grade class to become one of the premier pediatric neurosurgeons in the world. He got in touch with what was on the inside of him, shucked off the welfare environment and achieved great success. There are many others like him with great potential who are stuck in welfare, unable to see that on the inside they have what it takes to do outstanding things. But, once a captive of the welfare system, it is hard to get in touch with the power to claim life as the Creator intended it, and that is exactly what many politicians want.

Many politicians and poor people have developed an unhealthy, co-dependent relationship. Co-dependency is when there is a relationship in which a person is controlled or manipulated by another. What many people do not understand is that co-dependency affects both parties, making each dependent on the other for survival. Poor people are dependent on the gift of government money from democrats, so they, in order to continue receiving it, have no choice but to vote for them. The democrats, on the other hand, must give money to the poor so they will receive their votes. Neither these poor voters nor the democrats have the option of doing anything other than those things which will preserve their relationship. They are each controlled and manipulated by the other. We could say that each has the other dangling like a puppet on a string.

Poor people need to understand that the thrust of liberals is to get them fixed in a state of dependency. Intentionality is at the heart of this. The welfare program is geared toward doing just that. Once dependency is set, the liberals can count on the vote of unproductive poor people forever.

If we are to restore our constitutional form of government where people are expected to become producers, this co-dependency must end. All forms of subjugating others to one's dominance must cease. Slavery, no matter in what form it appears, must end. To be totally dependent on other people for sustenance is to be their slaves with little chance of breaking free.

POLITICIANS: DOWN WITH MENTAL HEALTH

Politicians are not interested in good, sound mental health for the American people. They will tell you they are, but the things they do indicate the opposite.

Many things can be said about the characteristics of good mental health. Following below are some of the more significant characteristics.

One of the things clients first present to mental health professionals is a poor opinion of themselves, expressing little confidence in their ability to emotionally care for themselves. When they learn to trust their counselors, they begin to tell of things other people have done which have led to their present feelings of poor self-worth.

Sarah was a college graduate and an accomplished pianist, and was a church choir director, accomplishments that would lead one to believe she thought highly of herself. The counselor used a scale of zero (0) to one hundred (100) for people to give a number indicating how good they felt about themselves, with zero being totally worthless and 100 being the best person who ever lived. This highly successful person was asked to give herself a number, and, after taking time to think, said, "I will give myself a five." With her background of significant accomplishments, this low number surprised the counselor.

This opened the door for expressions of feelings that had been hidden for years. She talked about the communication she and her sister had heard from their parents from their first memories. Both had been told by their parents over and over until they left home as teenagers that they were accidents and not wanted. The parental communication went something like this, "We did not want you and we did not want to take care of you. We had you, and we had to spend money on you, money we could have spent on ourselves. We wish you had never been born." The repetition of this over years was the basis of Sarah's tremendously bad feeling about herself. The memory was so powerful that Sarah's accomplishments did little to help her feelings of worthlessness.

If people do not feel good about themselves, it is difficult for them to have good, rewarding lives. They can accomplish a lot, but still feel bad about themselves. One of the main processes of therapy is helping people learn how to heal themselves, basing their opinions of themselves on themselves, not on the opinions of others, no matter who the others might be.

When people begin to build the foundation of their lives on their own thoughts and desires and a growing realization of the value placed on them by their Creator, they have the opportunity to begin shaping their environments on something far more stable than whatever comes from other people.

One of the reasons this section is titled, "Politicians: Down With Mental Health," is because politicians do not want people to be healthy enough to think for themselves. They know, when people learn to think for themselves, the time will come when they will realize the best life for them is one they build for themselves, not one given to them by someone else. Politicians want people to think the thoughts they are told to think. If they can accomplish this, the electorate will vote for them and assure their continued presence in office.

Courage is a characteristic of good mental health. The more healthy people become, the more likely they will face things in life and throw off the control others have over them. They will be able to look squarely at things and judge for themselves, not waiting for others to tell them what to think and do. It takes courage to build one's life on inner strengths and abilities when one's very existence has been previously controlled by others. Too many people take the easy road and give up thoughts of building the kind of life that comes from the inside. But, as people grow in mental health, they begin to build confidence in their ability to live as they determine.

Tenacity is another characteristic of good mental health. This is the ability to set one's course and go after it with grit and determination in order to succeed. Adversity, which comes to us all, is not seen as stopping our effort, but as something which is to be overcome in our process of becoming successful. Healthy people are not easily detoured from their destination. Politicians want to substitute, even force people toward, destinations they determine.

A desire to learn new things is characteristic of good mental health. Sitting down and shutting down your brain always leads to stagnation and decay. It is no wonder the quite attractive 28 year old was having trouble making good decisions when she reported having read only one book in her entire life. She had not prepared for an adult life because of her failure to exercise the brain God had given her. Life ceases to become better when we end our quest to learn new things. One of the things we can notice about poor people is their lack of interest in learning new things, and politicians are good at taking advantage of this.

High self-esteem is another characteristic of sound mental health. You believe in yourself and your ability to make a good life regardless of circumstances you might face. The "I can't do it," is not a part of your repertoire. The "I think I can; I think I can," which leads to "I know I can," is a central ingredient of a healthy person. Politicians do not want people to be healthy enough to believe in their ability to do well on their own initiative. They want them to believe they cannot get along without government assistance.

Good mental health includes doing things which are in our best interest. We don't do those things which are harmful to our bodies and minds. We respect the bodies and minds God has given us, seeing them as the best gift ever placed in our hands. We do not succumb to advertising which would have us believe we can't have a good life without purchasing the latest gizmos and gadgets or put into our bodies those things which dull our senses to where we can't take care of ourselves. This author works with people who continually choose things which are destroying their lives. Self-care is at the heart of good mental health. The message from Washington, however, is, "Do whatever you want to do, and we will pick you up."

Being responsible for what we do is another hallmark of good mental health. The young lady, after drinking 16 ounces of vodka, said, "It's not my fault I ran into the ditch. If the lady in front of me had not stopped, I would not have had to swerve to miss her. It was her fault." The mantra, "I am not responsible," reverberates throughout our society as people take no responsibility for their actions. Unfortunately, politicians love it when people flee their responsibilities because they then can step in and say, "Don't worry about it. We will take care of you; we will assume responsibility for what you do." One of the many places where they do this is telling men they do not have to be responsible for the children they father. The message out of Washington says to them, "We will pay physician and hospital expenses for your baby's delivery, and then, if you disappear, we will send the mother of your baby a check for care of the child." Quite often a couple with children will get a divorce, but still live together because the government will send a check to a single mother for care of the child. Yes, politicians are opposed to people assuming responsibility for what they do. When people do take responsibility for their lives, politicians can't control them with the checks from Washington.

Many other things can be said about good mental health, but this is enough to indicate that politicians are not interested in promoting good mental health because when people get to the place where they depend on themselves for a good life, they have no need for politicians.

One of the primary goals of mental health professionals is helping people heal themselves by gaining the ability to build their lives on their own decisions and what they can do for themselves.

OUR EDUCATIONAL SYSTEM:
AN ILLUSION OF KNOWLEDGE

Woodrow Wilson once said that the purpose of education was to teach people what do, how to do it, and when they are told to do it. There is no place in this for reason and creative thinking, leaving many of our graduates of public schools and colleges unable to negotiate life in a meaningful way.

The progressives in this country have followed Woodrow Wilson in building an educational system where students learn to do and think only what their mentors tell them to do and think. Education should be "the circumstance of apprehending truth or fact through reasoning" (Webster), but what we now have is a system in which students are taught to regurgitate what their teachers and professors give them. Students learn facts, figures, how to do certain jobs, and how to follow rules, but they do not have the ability to reason. This fully explains why the six year old girl could be sent to alternative school because the principal said the charm bracelet she wore could be used as a weapon, or the Eagle Scout was also sent to alternative school because he forgot to take a scout knife out of his car after attending a scout meeting the previous night, and this mandated the loss of a scholarship to one of the military academies. These principals have achieved their positions because they are "outstanding examples" of present-day educational leadership. How preposterous that they, devoid of the ability to rationally interpret rules and circumstances, are considered to be among the outstanding educational leadership in this country!!!

What our current educational system can be referred to is a system geared toward "dumbing" down the people in this country. This author is continually amazed at the inability of supposedly educated people to navigate through many troubling things in their lives. The exorbitant credit card debt run up by millions of people is an example of the inability of people to understand and deal with all the advertising of products and pleasures and allure of keeping up with the Joneses. Coming out of an educational background where they are told what to do, many people lack the ability to make decisions for themselves, becoming willing victims of those who all too willingly tell them they must have this or that thing in order to be happy.

In alcohol and drug classes, we talk about "playing the tape out." What this suggests is that we think through to the consequences of what we do, not end our thinking with the excitement and allure of a given moment. When people have been taught to do what they are told to do, they will be swayed by advertisers who are adept at convincing people they cannot live without their products. Our educational system well prepares people to be gullible to those who wish to get into our minds and bank accounts. Advertisers, politicians, religious people and others convince us that they have the secret to an enjoyable life, and take advantage of our inability to "play the tape out." We become gullible to promises which cannot be met, to dreams that can never come to fruition.

In the area of politics, we have seen in recent years another movement which is, in effect, leading people around by the nose, and many do not know what is happening to them. This sort of thing takes place when people look outside themselves for their savior rather than seeing their salvation coming from within themselves. The inability to reason and think was on full display when millions of people, supposedly well educated, voted for Mr. Obama after he promised to bring change, but they never bothered to examine the ramifications of what he said. Had they understood his words, they would have run from him like people run from a tornado. To give someone a job with no training for that job and no idea regarding what that job might be is sheer lunacy.

Our public educational system has not taught us to be contributors to the good of our country. It has prepared us to earn a living by giving the skills to do something over and over, but it has not given us the ability to think clearly and rationally about our part in maintaining and advancing our constitutional form of government. Too few of us understand that we are a part of the greatest nation ever to appear on the face of the earth, and our job is to contribute something good to it. Many people, rather than helping solve our problems, have chosen to concentrate on our negatives and go through life grumbling and complaining about what they do not have.

In the last three years, Mr. Obama has taken opportunity after opportunity to talk about the bad things in the United States, but has had little to say about what is good about our country, and he is cheered on by minds without the ability to understand the difficult process this nation has gone through to make freedoms available to everyone. These are the people who fail to believe in themselves and accuse others of causing their failures in life. "It's not my fault I have made nothing of my life; somebody else is responsible," is the cry of millions of people eager to blame others for their failures. They accuse other people of keeping them from taking advantage of opportunities offered in this country.

As a nation, we struggled many years to open opportunities for all citizens, but, in the last 60 years we have made it possible for everyone to get an education and achieve if they are willing to pay the price of achievement. We should remember that complaints alone are never the fuel of progress. They can set the stage for progress, but they must be followed by minds prepared to think and reason about the complexities inherent in building a great nation. Thoughtful development of solutions to the problems we face is necessary if progress is to be made. We need great minds if we are to continue building what our Founders started. Our educational system must be changed if we are to escape our susceptibility to those who promise to bring change, but have no ability to deliver what we need.

GOVERNMENT CAUSING ECONOMIC DISASTER

Our dollar is dying. On Tuesday, April 19, 2011, the following appeared in the Atlanta Journal/Constitution:

Debt Warning Sounds Alarm. With spending, revenue out of balance, S&P goes negative on U.S. The rating agency Standard and Poor's warned the United States on Monday that it could lose its coveted status as the world's most secure economy if lawmakers don't rein in the nation's nearly $14.3 trillion debt.

"S&P changed its outlook on the United States from "stable" to "negative" and said the federal government could lose its AAA rating if officials fail to bring spending in line with revenues."

On June 5, 2011 there was a quote of Chinese President Hu Jintao on internet news in which he said that the dollar dominated world is a "product of the past." On April 13, 2010, the Strategy, Policy and Review Department of the International Monetary Fund (IMF) recommended that the world adopt a global currency called the "Bancor." One argument for this is that the world needs a currency which is more stable than the dollar. With the dramatic decrease in the value of the dollar over the past few years, particularly the last three, good argument can be made for something more stable. One thing we should be aware of is that the Bancor would be administered by a global central bank, with the possibility that the U. S. would have little influence in determining exchange rates. With all the dollars the Federal Reserve has printed in recent years, this could prove troublesome to us.

On June 23, 2011 the following appeared on the internet, "The national debt will exceed the entire U.S. economy by 2021 - and balloon to nearly 200 percent of GDP within 25 years - without dramatic cuts to federal health and retirement programs or steep tax increases, congressional budget analysts said Wednesday."

We should see this is as clear indication that the politicians we have been sending to Washington don't have a clue regarding financial responsibility. The group there now seems to be the most clueless of them all. We now face a president and much of Congress not understanding what is happening, and, as a result, want to continue spending without restraint. They figure on doing what they have done in the past: take more and more money away from taxpayers to do lots and lots of things which do not need to be done.

We may be on the verge of the greatest economic calamity since the Great Depression, and it could even be worse. We are now being bombarded with voices about a possible return to something similar to the world in which I was born in the 1930's. **Politicians in Washington have done this to us.** They have been out of control, and, if significant changes are not soon made with how they handle taxpayer's money, that is exactly where we will go, and rather quickly. The word **"IRRATIONALITY"** is a word well-suited to their deliberations.

Since the early part of 2002, the value of our dollar has declined against major currencies by approximately 35 percent (as of May, 2011), and some economists are saying the decline is accelerating, with a decline during the last year of over 12 percent. As an example, I remember when I could have purchased an Euro for 79 cents. As of today when this is written, the Euro will cost me $1.40. This is dramatic, but the people in power now are giving signs of deliberately planning further decline in the value of our dollar. It is unfathomable that the president and his people would allow and/or cause this to happen.

Politicians want to solve all the problems of the world by extracting more and more money from the pockets of taxpayers. This has been going on for a long time, and, even though many of their programs are abject failures, they continue to persist in adding to these failures.

The Social Security Program begun by President Franklin Roosevelt is a great example of politicians attempting to solve a problem they could not solve. This writer and millions of other seniors are receiving benefits from this program, but the truth is, if I had been required to invest my money in a program of my own choosing, my monthly income would be significantly higher than it is right now. No politician can do for me what I can do for myself, and this runs true for everybody in the U. S. if they get a little professional advice and assistance. Rather than helping us older people, the SS program has actually hurt us. And, of course, as everyone knows, it will run out of money in just a few years. A program funded and owned by the American people would last as long as they lived.

The Great Society Program under President Lyndon Johnson was another colossal mistake by the politicians we sent to Washington. They assumed, incorrectly, that the War on Poverty would eliminate poverty, so they threw billions of taxpayer dollars to that end. But, poverty was not eliminated; it has been with us ever since, and it will remain with us. The problem is that a part of poverty is poverty of the mind. That's why people in my neighborhood who moved out of government housing and the ghettos into middle class housing still live as if they were back where they came from. The only thing that has changed is the house they live in. They don't pay their mortgages or the garbage bill or the car note (their cars still get repossessed), they still sell their drugs, in the yard across the street is a discarded air conditioner, a chair and other trash that has been there for at least two months, etc., etc.

The Major Great Society Programs were:
> War on Poverty
> Education
> Medicare and Medicaid
> National Endowment for the Arts and the Humanities
> Head Start

Many laws were passed during the Johnson Administration to promote these programs. Some of them have ended and some have been helpful to people with true need, but they have probably brought the greatest waste of economic and human wealth in the history of our country.

Since the Great Society Program, other laws from Congress are destroying our quality of life. A couple of examples will illustrate the pervasiveness of the damage they have done.

In a recent class, Joy, a woman in her mid to late 20's told about her sister, Susan, taking advantage of "free" money from Washington. Susan weighs over 300 pounds, and claimed disability because of her weight. The government sends her a check for being obese and unable to work. She talked a doctor into diagnosing her as bi-polar, so she receives a check for that. Joy said, "I have been around bi-polar people, and I can tell you she is not bi-polar." Being "bi-polar," the doctor wrote Susan a prescription for drugs. Joy said Susan, not really being bi-polar, does not take this medication, but sells it. She added, "The government is paying my sister to be a drug dealer." Susan, also, talked the doctor into diagnosing one of her children as bi-polar, and so more money and drugs are coming that way. She is also receiving a check for being a single mom, and she is pregnant with a third child. Thus, more money from Washington to pay for pre-natal care and delivery, to be followed by additional funds from Washington for care of the baby. Joy said Susan applied for food stamps, and "is receiving $1200 per month," and then added, "Why does anyone need $1200 a month for food?" Joy concluded her remarks about her sister by saying, "She is **not** disabled. She has a friend who cleans houses, and, if she ever needs more money, she works for her friend, and she has absolutely no trouble doing the work."

Multiply Susan's situation millions of times, and you can see the utter nonsense that is a part of what legislators and presidents do when they try to "take care" of people who should be taking care of themselves. To compound the problem, legislators did not provide a system to catch people like Susan, thus giving cheaters like her unlimited opportunities to participate in robbing those of us who pay taxes.

The second example relates to a letter I received in the mail yesterday. At the top of the letter is the name "Assurance Wireless," and the next words in bold print are, "A worry-free way to stay connected." I am addressed by name, followed by, "There's a way to stay in touch with family and friends for free." Further down are these words,: "How do you qualify? As a Georgia resident, you may qualify for Assurance Wireless if you participate in any of the following programs: Food Stamps, Medicaid, Supplemental Security Income (SSI), Low Income Home Energy Assistance Program (LIHEAP), Federal Public Housing Assistance (FPHA), Senior Citizen Low Income Discount Plan, Temporary Assistance for Needy Families (TANF)."

Many taxpayers in our country, many of them retired people who still pay taxes, cannot afford a cell phone, and, yet, they are being taxed to provide things like this for "poor" people.

These two examples tell us beyond a shadow of a doubt that the politicians in Washington have no clue regarding what they are doing to this nation or they are doing it deliberately to suck "poor" people into lives of dependency on politicians who will give them more and more. Either way, the politicians are using and abusing both the taxpayer **and** those who receive the "gov'ment" check.

Add to these things the Bail-out program, the biggest one-time waste of money in the history of this nation, the heavily flawed ObamaCare program, the Cash for Clunkers program, and many other things, and it is easily seen that, from an economic standpoint, legislators and the presidents are ruining this nation.

The American voter has no choice but to stop this nonsense at the ballot box or our entire economic and governmental system will collapse. A thought that comes to mind is: this could possibly be the intent of Obama and his group of advisors who wish to replace our system with a form of socialism they desire. Why else would they make such a mess of things? I prefer to believe incompetence is the basis for this.

The world is not rid, and never will be, of men who believe that everyone in the whole world will be better off if they are in charge. This is a delusion of vast proportions, but it is a delusion shared by too many men.

TYRANNY OF THE GOVERNMENT

It is apparent that the Washington crowd, chief among them being Mr. Obama, believe it is not only okay, but appropriate to force Americans to do what they do not want to do. They believe it is okay to force people to do things which make absolutely no sense. The Bail Out program was a boondoggle from the beginning, and most Americans strongly objected to it. We knew it would not do what they claimed it would do, and we knew it would force more dollars out of our pockets, so we opposed it. This made no difference to Obama and his democrats, so they paid no attention to us.

The healthcare legislation was another thing forced down our throats against our will. It was not read by those who voted for and passed it. Then Obama signed it, but he, too, did not read it. None of them knew what was in it, yet they passed it. This is sheer folly.

One of the things most of us are aware of is that dishonest people do not think like honest people. We, also, need to be aware that people who do not believe in constitutional government do not think like people who do believe in it. When they do not believe in it, which provides for representative government, they will not represent the people. By them not listening to the majority of us on several occasions, Obama and the democrats were saying loud and clear that they do not believe in constitutional government. If they do not believe in it, they should not be in Washington acting as if they know how to make this country go.

In late 2012 we will hold another election, and the voters will decide if we like what is going on in Washington or if we do not. Those who like the current governmental abuse of both the producers and the unproductive poor will vote to return those who are now there. Those who do not like to be abused by politicians will vote for people who understand that our government was set up to serve the people, not the people to serve government.

Under Mr. Obama's leadership, the federal government has made a mess of the immigration issue, having abandoned its responsibility to protect our borders, and, unbelievably, is suing Arizona for trying to do what the feds are supposed to do.

There is no question in this writers mind that Mr. Obama and the democrats are trying to install a socialist form of government against the will of the people. But, clear- thinking Americans know that no socialist form of government has ever come close to giving people opportunities for success like we have enjoyed Congress and previous presidents, without understanding what they were doing, forced a mortgage system on us that is **THE** cause of the economic meltdown. They forced lending institutions to lend money to people who had no jobs, no assets, absolutely nothing with which to repay their mortgages, and this has created disaster after disaster all across this country. Sensible Americans would have done nothing like this. We the People are too smart to do such a thing, but not the politicians in Washington. We know you cannot loan money to people without them having the ability to repay it, but the politicians did it anyway.

Lending institutions and some of the fat cats on Wall Street contributed to the mortgage mess, but the whole thing began when members of Congress and the president again tried to do something people should have the responsibility of doing for themselves.

What is going on in Washington is nothing other than an attempt to impose a way of life objected to by a majority of our citizens, but the politicians are paying no attention to us. This is nothing other than tyranny, and, if we leave the current legislators where they are, we will quickly reach the ultimate goal of tyranny, which is absolute power being invested in the hands of a single ruler, and, with his ego, Obama would love this. This is what we have been moving toward these last three years, and we voters are the only ones who will stop it.

Each person needs to be free to make his/her own way in this world. This freedom has been provided in no other country save our own. If tyranny takes hold, it will limit what can be achieved by an individual, group or our entire society. When anyone or any group thinks it is his/their duty to force a people to do things against their will, and people accept this, we have abandoned the purpose for which this nation was set up. Our Creator did not make us to be controlled by others, but to control our own lives. This is not possible with what is going on in Washington at the present time.

When a government, religion or any entity seeks to force its way, limitations of our God-given possibilities always follow. This is why all nations and individuals who practice tyranny will eventually fail.

One of the things politicians need to understand is that any attempt to force ones way upon another always creates resistance and a desire to get even. We are now seeing a strong emergence of resistance among productive people, and it will not end until politicians cease their efforts to subjugate us to their tyranny or we replace them all. If poor people understood what politicians are doing to them, they, too, would vote to remove the current bunch from office. Slowness of Americans to recognize the intent of our current politicians has placed us all in jeopardy of losing our constitutional form of government and the freedoms which go with it.

Unfortunately, we have many citizens who would welcome a tyranny if the tyrant put food in their mouths. This frees them from having to do it themselves. These are the kind of people who now have abandoned all efforts to care for themselves and have placed their future in the monthly welfare check. For productive people to fail to resist is a guarantee of disaster, for tyranny always works to have total control of people. The only way for us to maintain freedom is to endure against what Washington is now trying to do to us. Resisting with endurance may be costly, but it is the only way to freedom and wholeness.

When anyone turns control of his life over to another, his life is diminished. Living the dreams of another always means the loss of our own dreams. We were made to work, struggle if necessary, to give ourselves the good life, not the kind of life given to us by others. If the politicians now in Washington have their way, our lives will be diminished even further as they tell us what to do, how to do it, and when they want us to do it. If this day comes, we will have lost all our freedoms.

This writer does not believe this day will come because there are still enough strong Americans who understand what freedom is all about to resist and persist as long as needed.

CHAPTER FOUR

PRODUCTIVE AMERICANS & OBAMA'S LEADERSHIP

American voters did not pay enough attention to what Mr. Obama said he would do if he became president. He made his intentions quite clear on a Meet the Press program on September 7, 2008. General Bill Ginn (USAF ret.) asked him to explain why he doesn't follow protocol when the National Anthem is played. "Senator" Obama replied, "As I've said about the flag pin, I don't want to be perceived as taking sides."…."There are a lot of people in the world to whom the American flag is a symbol of oppression."…."The anthem itself conveys a war-like message. You know, the bombs bursting in air and all that sort of thing."…."The National Anthem should be swapped for something less parochial and less bellicose. I like the song 'I'd Like to Teach the World To Sing.' If that were our anthem, then I might salute it. In my opinion, we should consider reinventing our National Anthem as well as redesign our flag to better offer our enemies hope and love. It is my intention,, if elected, to disarm America to the level of acceptance to our Middle East Brethren. If we, as a nation of waring people, conduct ourselves like the nations of Islam, where peace prevails…perhaps a state or period of mutual accord could exist between our governments…"

These are some of the most preposterous, bazaar, and uninformed words to ever come out of the mouth of a man running for the highest office in the land. It indicates a basic, fundamental and naive misunderstanding of the history of the United States, the reason we exist as a nation, and the purpose we have as a free nation. For him to not understand that our flag is a symbol of freeing ourselves from the oppression of England is beyond reason. It appears that he does not have the capacity to see the good things of our nation, and the fact that the good things far outweigh the bad.

He said that peace prevails in the nations of Islam. He doesn't know what he is talking about. He apparently is ignorant of the history of the Middle East, the history of a religious people who have often been ruthlessly cruel to nations they have gone to war against. The Muslim world has been and is now working for the destruction of Israel; there is no question about this. Can Mr. Obama be so ill-informed and naïve as to be unaware that Mohammed and his successors started offensive wars so they could impose Islam by force on peaceful nations, which they did on all of North Africa, Iraq, Egypt, Iran, and other countries in the Middle East? He should read where Mohammed spoke of God ordering him to fight with people until they believed there was no God but Allah and that Mohammed was his messenger. Perhaps he thinks a "Holy War for the sake of God" is a way to bring peace. Many people have been deluded throughout history into believing that killing in the name of God is okay. Nothing could be further from the truth.

Muslims, by declaring "infidels" to be worthy of death, have given themselves permission to attack and kill any who do not accept the Koran the way they think it ought to be accepted. This is on the same level as Pope Urban II declaring in 1092 AD that it is the will of God for "Christian" soldiers to go into Palestine and yell, "It is the will of God," as they swing their swords and kill Muslims. The Christian Church has accepted the fact that this is a total misrepresentation of God, and some day the Muslims will do the same. A religion like this is not good for the world, and, long-term, it cannot endure.

For their religion to label all people who do not accept the Koran as "infidels" and worthy of being killed places all non-Muslims in a war zone where they are looked upon as deserving to be killed. Then, for Mr. Obama to see the celebration of the Muslim world following 9/11 and not recognize the evil therein further indicates his inability to know things as they really are. He does not need to look at ancient history to understand that the Muslim people are no better at bringing justice to the world than are other peoples and nations. Just the mention of men like Saddam Hussein, Omar Gaddafi, and the current ruthless leaders of Syria and Iran, plus other Muslim leaders is enough to identify them as on an equal footing with other evil men of history.

To say "he wants to disarm America to the level of acceptance to our Middle Eastern Brethren" is a statement signifying his belief that who and what we are should be determined by someone or some nation other than ourselves. To put the American people down this way is beyond comprehension. He does not believe in America and wishes to do away with who we are. He verbally claims to be a Christian, but, at heart, seems to be far more committed to the Muslim faith than he is to the Christian faith.

How did the American voters not see these things in the candidate Obama? This writer was mystified by this, being able to come up with only one explanation, and that is the inability of Americans to reason and think, which is a powerful commentary on the failure of the public educational system in our country. There is no way a thinking person can compare our Constitutional Republic with any other system in the world and think there is something better. The judgment of the world is that we have the best system of government ever devised by man, and many other nations have used our Constitution as a pattern in the development of their own governing documents. The fact that more people want to immigrate to the United States than to any other country is recognition that we have the best nation yet. Mr. Obama has no appreciation of this, whatsoever.

One of the marks of an intelligent people is their readiness to question, reason and think about things presented to them. The American people did not do this when Mr. Obama said, in effect, that he wanted us to become like Islamic nations, that he was going to disarm us to a level acceptable to the Muslims. The care and direction of this nation are not in the hands of a president. The Constitution says ultimate power is in the hands of the people. We let down our guard, and Mr. Obama and his advisors came along and began running the government without concern for the provisions of the Constitution. Mr. Obama interpreted his election as a license to do anything he wishes to do, and he has done just that without paying attention to the greatest governmental document in recorded history. If we voters do not accept our role in preserving our nation, Mr. Obama and his people will destroy it, being cheered on by a great host of liberals, many of whom are democrats.

This writer was amazed when Obama was chosen, first, as the democratic candidate for president, and, second, utterly amazed when the American voters elected him as president. The second time I heard him speak while campaigning, I interpreted what he said as indicating his desire was to become a dictator. Nothing he has done or said since has caused me to change my mind. Not only that, but it would not surprise me to learn that he wants to be king of the world, which is a problem many previous leaders around the world have had.

When Mr. Obama took the oath of office and swore to defend and protect the Constitution of the United States, he had no intention of doing this. This puts him in the category of one who tells things other than the truth, which, some people would say, makes him a liar. Grasping power and ignoring the Constitution are not actions acceptable to the American people.

When we elect those we send to Washington, we elect them to do what is in the best interest of the country as a whole, and the rights of the nation are what the citizens determine them to be. The government cannot force citizens as a whole to do what they do not want to do. The Founders were fully aware that power vested in a single individual or group could easily lead to tyranny, as has so often been the case throughout history. This is **the reason** they placed ultimate authority in the hands of the people. Viewed against the backdrop of history, this was a miraculous achievement.

We have had politicians and presidents in the past who have struggled to understand this ultimate power in the hands of the people, but, up until now, no president has taken it upon himself to so completely ignore the Constitution and wishes of the people. It is apparent that Mr. Obama believed his election authorized and empowered him to disregard the wishes of the American people and do whatever he decides to do, and his fellow democrats have supported and cheered him on.

He was elected to move us closer to the ideals of freedom and liberty inherent in a Constitutional Republic, moving us further toward provision of equality of opportunity for all. He has not done this, having generated more division between the producers and the non-producers than this writer has witnessed in his 70 plus years of life.

Dishonest people do not think like honest people, non-Christians do not think like Christians; non-Muslim people do not think like Muslims. For this reason Mr. Obama does not think in the context of constitutional government and can easily disregard what a president of the United States is supposed to do, doing whatever he wants to do. Ignoring the wishes of the people is not possible under our form of government. Once an individual sets out on the journey of ignoring the people, he will not stop until he is made to stop.

From the beginning of his presidency he has failed. Most people are aware that, whenever new leadership comes to an organization, that organization begins to immediately show signs of improvement - that is, if the leadership is good. We have not seen improvement, but continued deterioration of our nation in many areas since Mr. Obama became president. He has set us on a course that will complete the demise of America if we voters don't correct it. **We have reached a time when many citizens are giving thought to what they must do to protect themselves from the politicians in Washington.** This is a deplorable situation that should never exist in a Constitutional Republic, and, if we citizens do not exercise our ultimate power, our nation will be taken away from us by a man who would be king.

It is a wonder we have not heard rumblings from the earth as the founders of our nation have rolled over in their graves regarding what is going on in the Oval Office and Congress. They would be shocked to know those now in power are grounded in liberalism, socialism and communism, three philosophies that are foreign to the kind of government they set up. This is a group we might refer to as the **Tripartite Gang** in the Oval Office. They are a group of people who have come together to dramatically alter the way we do things in this country, and, if they are successful, they will certainly bring about the death of this great nation.

This **Tripartite Gang** thinks it knows a better way than constitutional government and the free enterprise system. The system they want to install has never worked as well as what we have been building. They fail to understand that laws are made to feed the rights of people, not take them away. For some time, liberals, mostly democrats, have been attempting to make citizens dependent on them rather than on themselves. But, most Americans know that the only life worth living is the one we make for ourselves. Dependency on others to call the shots always leads to abandonment of our purpose for living.

This **Tripartite Gang** of liberals, socialists, and communists has already made great strides in condemnation of capitalism and the free enterprise system, and are doing their best to spread productive people's wealth among those who have no right to have it. They have been busy transferring jobs from our people to other nations, i.e. loaning Brazil $2 billion to drill deep water oil wells off their coast while not permitting Americans to do the same in the Gulf. They have found ways to extract more money from our pockets, i.e. the bail-out program, Obama Care, the Cash for Clunkers programs, etc., etc. They have guaranteed the continuing transfer of our gas money to oil-producing countries, i.e. by disallowing drilling where we know oil exists in Alaska and other parts of our nation, thus guaranteeing our continuing dependence on foreign oil. They have managed to intensify class warfare by communicating to the poor that they have every right to live off the labor of the producers in this country. They have used taxpayer money to bail out Greece, another indication that Mr. Obama is more interested in the welfare of people from other countries than the citizens of the United States.

Our main job in relationships with each other is to learn to live together, and our government is not helping us do this. On the contrary, it is doing things which divide us, things which have created the biggest class warfare in my time on earth. Our failure to learn to live together is seen in the many ways we hurt each other, perhaps best manifested in the wars we have fought. Instead of seeing our differences as opportunities to solve problems, we see them as occasions to take up arms against and kill each other. Government is out of order when it develops programs that generate division among us, but many of Obama's programs do just that.

We have far more good things coming out of capitalism than has ever come out of any other system. Mr. Obama cannot see this because he has been brainwashed by mentors without an understanding and appreciation of our way of life. Capitalism does not guarantee wealth for everyone, but it does make it available to anyone who is willing to pay the price for success, which includes study, discipline, hard work, and a dogged determination to succeed. Capitalism is built on the belief that people are capable of taking care of themselves. Socialism/communism is built on the belief that people are not able to care for themselves, and, thus, need government.

This gang in Washington believes they can correct problems in the Middle East, i.e. Obama's becoming one with the Arabs in their struggles against Israel. This is nothing other than living in a dream world. In his efforts to be popular with the Arab world, he has positioned himself with those who desire the extermination of the Jewish people. He is trying to sell himself as a good guy to peoples of other nations, and, like he has fooled many people in the U. S., he has many of them fooled, but they, like our citizens, will learn that his actions do not match his words.

This **Tripartite Gang** either does not know what it is doing or it is deliberately dividing the people of this country. Things they touch in the United States are not getting better, but far worse, but they persist in what they are doing.

Mr. Obama sees through a glass darkened by the virulence of men like Rev. Wright, who was pastor of what was called a Christian church, but who showed little to no signs of understanding that Christianity is all about love, not the hatred he spewed out on our nation and people. For 20 years Obama was exposed to a brand of religion that permits abuse of power and people, which is not possible in true Christianity. Twenty years of this was bound to have a lasting negative effect.

It is not unusual for people to claim to be Christian and have no idea what it is all about. Claiming to be Christian while retaining the right to be ruthless and destructive in their treatment of people cannot be a part of Christianity. Wherever people claim to be Christian, but do things which diminish the lives of other people, we know right then and there that they do not understand what being a Christian is all about.

As previously stated, when people say they believe in something, they act like they believe it. We now have a bunch of people in the Oval Office who are doing things that give no recognition of belief in things that have made us a great nation. Obama's philosophy of life was built at the feet of people without appreciation for the accomplishments of this country, people like his professors, the Hyde Park crowd and a family marked with great dysfunction. These people left him with concepts that have no place in a constitutional government, the free enterprise system, and a nation that attributes much of its success to God.

Another mark of a good leader is **readiness to act** when action is necessary. Obama was not ready to make necessary decisions in the Gulf Oil Crisis, where delay in accepting the help of other nations led to far more damage than should have been experienced. As referenced earlier, he would not let American companies drill in the Gulf, but sent $2 billion to Brazil to help them drill, thus transferring 50,000 jobs and profits out of the United States. He was slow to react to the tsunami and nuclear disaster in Japan, thus slowing the assistance we could give them. He failed to take action in Libya when it was first needed, when the rebels had the upper hand, and this delay has cost hundreds if not thousands of lives and much wealth. Then he turned over to the countries in Europe a job that only America was equipped and prepared to do. Further, many in Congress believe he violated the War Powers Act by what he did, and, of course, he is disregarding their concern about this..

Obama's foreign policy is at best confused, erratic and inadequate. He is destroying our credibility as the leader of the free world, saying we should "lead from behind." This is another strong indication of his failure to understand what leadership is all about. No person standing in the middle or back of the line has much to say about where the line will go. That decision is made by the person or people out front. We need to pay attention when an Arab leader says, "The United States doesn't matter anymore," or when the Chinese president says to the people of Southeast Asia, "You should not be concerned about the power of the United States." Obama is seriously diminishing our status of being the leader of the world. It leads this writer to question his sense of adequacy and that of his advisors to be the leaders the United States and the world need at this time.

He has failed to act in small things. What should have been a simple, uncomplicated problem to resolve gives excellent commentary on his inability to lead. There has been tremendous "distraction" regarding his birth certificate, and it did not have to be. He had within his power from the beginning to eliminate the problem, that is if he has a genuine birth certificate. All he had to do was release it and the controversy would have died. A very simple act that would have taken no more than a few hours, but he did not do it, allowing the distraction to grow larger. No good leader will allow such a simple thing to cause so much controversy and dissension when he can easily do something about it. Could it be that he has allowed this controversy to continue so people will pay less attention to his record of failure in so many other things?

Mr. Obama and the democrats have used our tax money to bribe unions, AARP, politicians in their own party, and others for the purpose of buying support of the healthcare legislation. Unfortunately, bribery is not unknown in Washington, but it has never been good. Taking our tax money and using it in this way is out and out theft. We productive people did not pay our taxes for that purpose. It furthers their own ends, having nothing to do with what is best for America. This kind of corruption might be acceptable in Chicago gangster politics, but it has no place in the Oval Office and on Capitol Hill. We tax payers send money to IRS to be used for the good of all Americans, not private organizations serving a small percentage of our people. Too much of this has been done in the past, and it is time for it to stop.

A fundamental error made by Mr. Obama and his advisors is their belief that the source of life for a nation lies in the minds of those who are its leaders as they determine what life shall be for all citizens. This is where our founders were leaps and bounds ahead of them. They recognized that the source of life for individuals and a nation lies with God. Kicking God out of the deliberations in government limits the freedom and happiness humans can achieve. Happiness is the goal of life for people, but it does not come in the form of a "gov'ment" check or control from those in power. Humans need to be empowered to find their own way to a happy life, but this never comes so long as others determine what life will be for us.

In regard to the economy, Mr. Obama has stumbled and fallen, with many of his policies being abject failures. He and his people have done the wrong things. They labor under a fundamental misunderstanding of what makes our economy go. We have not had a great economy in the past few years because of what legislators and presidents have done. We have had a great economy because of what American businesses and citizens do, and the recent collapse of the economy can be laid squarely at the feet of those people we elected and sent to Washington to take care of our country. They have failed miserably, bringing us to the place where we can refer to the current economic crisis as a "Steep Recession."

Our failing economy has gotten worse since Mr. Obama took office. As suggested earlier, whenever a new leader comes to a troubled organization, that organization always begins to get better. The success of this leader, who must take what is handed him, is judged by what he does from that moment on, not on what other people have done up to that point. Success or lack of success cannot be blamed on what has gone on before. A poor leader will point his finger at his predecessors as the cause of failure, and Mr. Obama has done a superb job of blaming his failures on them.

When a trauma patient is brought into an emergency room, a doctor gets busy using all available skills to save the life of the patient and do things which allow the body to heal itself. He does not spend time ruminating over what caused the trauma. That would be a waste of time, and the delay in treatment might result in an unnecessary death. A doctor may not even be concerned about what caused the trauma; his interest is in saving the life of the patient. He looks forward, not backward, doing what is necessary for the welfare of the patient.

Politicians need to learn that their job is not to heal our economy. This is something they cannot do as indicated by the failure of the bailout programs and other things. Their job is to do those thing which allow the American people to heal the economy. The only way for our economy to again become robust is for politicians to empower the business world and the citizens to do what only they can do, and then get out of our way.

Another analogy might be appropriate. In the NFL world, the rules-makers and the referees know they should not jump into the game and play. That would be a disaster and some of them might get killed. In like manner, the politician's job is to make the rules and do the refereeing, but allowing the players, the businesses and citizens, to do the things they know how to do. What we need from politicians are the rules that make things fair to all and which protect us from those who would hurt, cheat and steal from us. By them jumping in and trying to play the game, they are the ones who have hurt, cheated and stolen from us in order to do things which are not in the best interest of this country.

When we look at the things Obama has said, and the things he has done since being in office, we need to ask, "What do his words mean, and what is suggested by his actions?" An intelligent electorate would have asked serious questions about his words during the campaign process, but did not do so, indicating an inability on the part of the American people to reason and think about the intentions of an office-seeker. It has become abundantly clear that Obama has no intention of being a president under the guidelines of the Constitution of the United States, and we voters should have picked that up. The only guideline he follows is what he wants, which frees him to do anything that comes to mind.

CHAPTER FIVE

STEPS TO RESTORE OUR NATION

If we are to restore constitutional government and our free enterprise system, there are many things we must do. One of the first will be to help people understand the differences between life under our constitutional government and life under socialism. Our constitutional government gives people freedom to be and do whatever they wish. Socialism offers people an opportunity to do and be what is determined by politicians, and places one's income at the disposal of those who decide what the limits of your life will be. Those who like to receive the handout from Washington taken from productive people will resist any change back toward the freedoms we have enjoyed for so long. Having allowed politicians to take us where our Forefathers never intended, we must be ready to work and, if necessary, suffer in order to continue our march toward freedom and equality for all citizens. Those who believe in socialism will hold tenaciously to the idea that a society functions best when the means of production are owned and controlled by the State, which, in effect, means loss of freedom for all citizens.

It was not easy for our founders to form a nation that gave power to its citizens, something never before done in any country throughout the history of the world, but what they did resulted in us becoming a nation of exceptionalism. Our current leaders have no clue regarding what this exceptionalism is all about. When Obama says our exceptionalism is no different from the exceptionalism of other countries, we must ask, "Where has he been that he does not understand this?"

Knowing where to start in dealing with the great deterioration of our nation is difficult because there are so many things that need to be done. What is presented in the following part of this book covers only some of the things needing our attention.

FACING OUR DENIAL

In the field of alcohol and drug addiction, one of the things clients must do before they can make progress toward health is to accept the reality that they are addicted. Until this is done, there is little hope they can stop drinking and using, sometimes even making the drug.

John and Sarah came for counseling. They had a three year old child and wanted another, but Sarah advised John she was not having another child until he quit making, selling and using his methamphetamine. During the first session he said, "I don't have a problem. There is nothing wrong with me making meth, selling it and using it myself. It's not hurting me in any way and it is giving us more money to spend." He went on to say that it was helping him because, when he was taking it, he could get more things done. "I can come home on Friday from work, start taking it and I can stay up all night doing things. Then the next day I can go hunting, hunt all day and night and the next day, come home on Sunday evening, go to bed and get up the next day and go to work. There aren't many people who can do anything like that." It mattered not to him that he was neglecting his family while taking meth. He was in total denial about his problem and had no interest in doing something about it

Over the next several weeks, he remained adamant, refusing to face the truth about himself. It took the second intervention by his family for him to face his addiction. They got his attention when they said, "You agree to enter a rehab program tomorrow or we will take you to jail tonight." He got the message and entered the program. Six years later he remains clean. Change was impossible so long as he was in denial, but good things happened when he "fessed up" to his addiction.

The Congress and the presidents of the United States have been addicted to spending money for a long time, and many of them have been and are in total denial that they have done anything wrong. Even now, June, 2011, in the midst of serious deliberations regarding raising the debt level only if there is significant reductions in spending, Obama and most of the democrats are trying to hold onto their spending habits.

We are being told a serious shutdown of the government will be a catastrophe if the debt level is not raised. But, would this be a worse catastrophe than the current catastrophe we are already experiencing with our spending problems? Some estimates are that each family in the U. S. has a debt of $524,000 for unfunded programs. To face this and honestly deal with it might give the American people an opportunity to replace legislators who have caused the mess.

Many of our citizens are in denial about what is going on in Washington, encouraging politicians to do more of what has brought the financial storm we are now in. In so many words, unproductive citizens continue to say, "I don't care what's happening to our country. Just give me more and more and more. What I get is the only thing that is important."

There is no economic hope for our nation if liberal politicians keep spending as they have done in the past, and if unproductive citizens continue their grasp for "free" money from Washington. Knowing that humans have difficulty changing their ways of doing things, we voters cannot allow many of the current members of Congress and Mr. Obama to remain where they are. They will keep doing what they have done, and, as the motivational speaker from Texas said, "If you keep on doing the things you have done, you will keep on getting the things you've got" (not good English, but the meaning is clear).

TERM LIMITS: ESSENTIAL FOR OUR NATION

If we are going to salvage this country for now and the future, it is imperative that we establish term limits. What we have now is a system that encourages politicians to put personal survival in Washington at the top of their priority list. It is not to do what is in the best interest of our nation. As a result, their primary job becomes that of convincing people to vote for them, and their actions are directed to that end. This is why the liberal element has chosen to "take care" of poor people because they know poor people can be sucked into their net through the gift of money taken from successful people. This is why politicians spend so much time and money on the campaign trail trying to convince people to vote for them. If they were doing their jobs of providing what is best for our nation, the people would fully recognize this and vote for them without having to be smoozed to and lied to. This suggests that the welfare of the nation as a whole is not of much concern to either the liberal politician or the poor person. They scratch each other's backs, and the result is a lifetime of politicians receiving votes and poor people receiving the monthly "gov'ment" check. Neither is particularly interested in committing to those things which enhance life in a Constitutional Republic.

We should all participate in building and developing this nation so it becomes a better place for all citizens, not just a select group. We do need to ask the question, "What is in my best interest?," but we must realize that what is in my best interest long-term does not include discriminating against or hurting other people in any way. We fail to understand this and go our way thinking it is okay to use other people any way we wish in order to enhance our own lives. This creates animosity and bad relationships which seriously limit our ability to live together and provide freedom and equality for all.

The strong message coming out of our current administration and Congress is that it is okay to hurt people if it will help me do **what I want to do.** With this being the basis of decision-making, there is no chance that the welfare of the entire nation is of concern.

The lies, deal-making, discrimination in the use of the Bail-out money, the bribery and many of the programs which take from producers and give to the non-producers are ample evidence that the group of politicians we now have in Washington is not in the best interest of our entire nation. The buying and selling of votes is at the heart of the welfare system, and is the reason so many people, many of them politicians, have become useless in making us a better nation.

Term limits would put an end to this. There would be no need for politicians to buy votes because, going home at the end of their term limit, they would not be on the ballot to receive those votes, and there would be no merit in politicians promising to give gifts to the unproductive/poor because they would not be in office to do so.

If the practice of scratching each others backs ended, politicians would have enough time to develop programs for the benefit of all Americans, and poor people would have no choice but to learn to take care of themselves, which is what all good citizens do. Living off the sweat and labor of productive people would have to be replaced with living off their own sweat and labor, which would bring them a far better life than can be provided by the establishment in Washington.

We have no choice but to replace the people in Washington who have brought our economic disaster. It does not matter where they come from, what the color of their skin is or any other thing. If they are a part of dragging our nation down, they must go; we have no other option. Their replacements must be competent enough to understand that spending more money than taken in always leads to bankruptcy, and they must understand that the Constitution is the document on which this country was founded and exists. This does not seem to be the case with those who have been at the helm of our government for decades, so one of the things we can say about them is that they are economically incompetent and willfully ignorant of constitutional government, even some who have degrees in law, business and accounting. Too many people have pieces of paper from prestigious educational institutions hanging on walls which mean absolutely nothing.

This author never made a lot of money in the not-for-profit field, but what the politicians in Washington have done in the last 20 years has reduced my assets by at least $150 thousand (my house and a few savings included). I had nothing to do with this reduction. Politicians did it to me. All my acquaintances tell me the same things has happened to them. This makes politicians worthy of being sent home, never to return again.

BEEFING UP REQUIREMENTS

If we're going to salvage this nation, we voters have got to do better than we have done in the past. Our standards have been far too low, and we have elected some individuals who are scoundrels, some with too little sense to do the job we have sent them to do, many who are terribly dysfunctional, and some who are out-and-out criminals. We have allowed them to use and abuse us, and it is time we put a stop to what they have done to us. We are not here for them to pilfer money from our pockets to fund any wild-haired idea they might have.

Okay, where have we fallen short, and what must we require of those who will represent us? This is only a brief look at things our country needs.

1. Politicians who have participated on putting this country on its knees must go. We have experienced the deep damage done to our country for decades, but especially in these last three years by those who wish to disregard the Constitution and replace it with socialism. It is reasonable that anyone running for office should be required to accept the Constitution as the basis of our government. If an individual cannot do this, he/she should not be put on the ballot.

2. Politicians must support the Free Enterprise System. This system, with its promise that, if you work hard and are successful, you can receive your deserved rewards, is the best system ever devised for a nation. There has never been a better way to build an economy and reward people for their labors. Taking from the rich and giving to the poor, a main characteristic of socialism, is a certain way of limiting achievement by hard-working people and trapping poor people in a life of dependence where they can never enjoy the kind of life they deserve. The free enterprise system, with its rewards for achievement, has produced wealth far above that of any other system. It has led to the American business

leaders and workers being on the forefront of developments in business, science, discovery, and many other things.

3. We must elect politicians who are aware that something beyond human wisdom is needed if they are to lead us further on the road to equality and freedom for all. The events of the past few years make quite clear the inadequacy of things done by men and women who rely completely on their own wisdom for guidance. The Founders of our nation recognized their dependence upon God, not upon religion, in their work of creating this greatest of nations. Our return to greatness will involve a similar recognition.

4. Politicians must understand that a nation is not built by dividing people. The reason we were so successful in World War Two is because we were united around a common cause. Nothing that has been coming out of Washington these past three years comes anywhere close to uniting us around a common cause. Rather, it has been the genesis of division and anger that has never before existed with my peers. If we cannot come together under a common cause, we have no chance of continuing the growth of our great nation.

5. We must replace the welfare system, one that takes the very life out of people, and replace it with an incentive-based system that allows people to build lives far superior to anything possible with the "gov'ment" check.

6. Our educational system must be changed. The U. S. Department of Education became a cabinet level department in 1979 under Jimmy Carter. It does a lot of good things, but, compared to education in other countries, it has not done its primary job of improving the educational level of our people. Our students have fallen behind students from other countries. Instead of people being trained to do what they are told to do the way they are told to do it and when they are told to do it, they must be given the tools to reason and think about things. This is the only way for people to begin questioning the limitations others, particularly politicians, place on them, thus limiting their ability to build the kind of life that is right for them. It may be time to consider returning responsibility for education back to the states.

7. We must again learn what the word 'morality' means, which is defined by Webster as "the principles of right and wrong in behavior." If we apply this definition to what politicians in Washington are doing, we have a huge problem. In a free society, no-one has the right to impose his will upon another so long as this other person is a law-abiding citizen, but politicians do this all the time. They are skilled at doing the wrong thing.

Some people take the position that it is okay to do the wrong thing if it will produce a higher good, but what some people think is the higher good is not that at all. Liberals/socialists/communists think it is moral to take from the haves and give to the have-nots so the have-nots can enjoy a better quality of life. In a Constitutional Republic, people interpret such action as immoral because it takes unreasonable amounts of money away from productive people, but, equally, it puts poor people in a state of dependency that leads them to being useless in our efforts to become a better nation. Both of these things are wrong.

On the individual level, we have lost sight of the difference between right and wrong. We have convinced ourselves that the chief good in life is to pursue hedonism, which is defined as "the doctrine that pleasure is the sole or chief good in life." As a result, we have gotten to the point where bazaar and destructive behavior is an acceptable, even preferred, way of life. Our chief goal has become doing what feels good. This is a distinct moral problem because it removes us from having to give any thought to doing the right thing. If we do not give thought to doing the right thing, the sky is our limit in any activity that feels good.

An appropriate question to ask is, "Have we become blind to what is right and wrong both as individuals and as a nation?" If we answer this on the basis of the things portrayed on the movie screens, our T.V. sets, the internet, the dysfunction we see in our "leaders," the number of people we have perpetrating crimes and occupying jail/prison cells, etc., etc., it appears we come up way short of being a moral nation.

In the coming 2012 election, we voters are faced with the question, "What is the right thing for us to do to restore the best form of government the world has ever known?" This is indeed a moral question.

GETTING RID OF DOGS

One of the things successful business leaders have learned is the necessity of getting rid of departments and programs which are not contributing to the good of the organization. Some people refer to this as "getting rid of the dogs."

We have a lot of "dogs" not carrying their own weight in our federal government, departments which are contributing virtually nothing to the good of our nation while costing taxpayers an arm and a leg. Efforts have been made in the past to eliminate some of these unneeded programs, but "politics" have kept them alive. Politicians have refused to do their job of running an efficient government.

There are many "dogs" needing swift termination, but only one will be mentioned. A brave soul could be given the job of identifying others.

The Internal Revenue Service is a department that must go. The budget for the year 2010 was $12.1 billion, an increase of over $600 million the previous year. One of its jobs is enforcement, catching those who avoid taxes.

We need a system where people could not avoid taxes when they purchase anything. Most businesses now collect state sales tax, so switching over to this would be relatively simple. It would close the possibility of people learning how to beat the system, with some of them being caught and thrown into jail at taxpayer's expense. It would collect tax from all the illegal immigrants in this country (the man I met last week earning $50 K per year, but with no Social Security card or Green Card would pay taxes when he bought things). The loopholes in current tax law would disappear. People, rather than politicians, would decide how much tax they would pay, knowing that any purchase made would require a tax. If they did not want to pay the tax, they just simply would not buy the product.

It would probably come as a shock to all of us if we learned the extent and cost of programs in our federal government that are simply not needed and are a huge waste of our money. We need a reasonable, systematic approach to getting rid of all the "dogs" in Washington. It will take someone with a tough skin to tackle this problem. Much more could be said about this, but this is sufficient at this time.

A JOURNEY AVAILABLE FOR ALL

Everyone needs to experience the "Aha" moment in life, a time when we realize we amount to something and have a purpose for living. When this moment happens, we are poised to begin a journey that leads toward success in life and the true happiness for which we yearn.

When we arrive at this "Aha" moment, we begin to have a passion for life, one which brings realization that life is far more than money, power or accumulation of things. But, more than passion is required, for passion un-tempered with wisdom and understanding can bring us to ruin. That is one of the great lessons of history. This wisdom and understanding take us beyond the mind of men to where we can be free from the encroachments of anyone or anything beyond us. It is our responsibility to act in accordance with who we are and what is on the inside of us, not in accordance with what other people want for us, no matter who they might be.

We have a tendency to look for a savior to appear and take us to where we want to go, giving us the longings of our hearts, but that never happens. Individual happiness and fulfillment cannot be put in a box or in a check and given to us. It must come from deep within where we find the capability of determining what our life will be.

When we put human wisdom at the top of the totem pole, we cannot rise above the limitations of our minds. We have seen the results of this as legislators have passed laws which have no place in our form of government. We can truly use the word 'irrationality' when referring to many of the things they have done. With irrationality having become the basis of deliberations on Capitol Hill and in the Oval Office, our way of life has been declining for many years.

What our founders gave us, when set against the backdrop of history, may well-qualify as a miracle because it allowed us to build our lives according to our own wishes, something socialism, communism, kings and dictators never allow. The result has been that productive people in this country have achieved marvelous things, and take great pride in calling themselves "American." There has never been another people quite like us in our achievements. Unfortunately, our government, over the last 60 years, but particularly over the last three years, has succeeded in diminishing this pride for most of us.

To say we are the greatest nation in history is not to minimize the problems we have had and do have. There is still much that needs to be done. We have solved many problems, and we will solve others, knowing there will never be a time when we are perfect. With the resources we have, primarily our good people, we will solve things which limit individual achievement and happiness, and, thus, the achievement and happiness of our entire nation.

Irrationality never brings good things. In our free society, it is not rational to deny people the right to self-determination, but legislation from Capitol Hill often subjugates people, without them even knowing what is happening, to a form of utter dependency, which is nothing other than intellectual and emotional slavery. We should be free in all respects to pursue our dreams. We fought the Civil War to remove physical slavery, but we now face the task of protecting ourselves from the politicians in Washington, those who would subject us to the slavery of dependence on them instead of on ourselves.

The can-do attitude of the 1940's and 1950's has been seriously eroded. We came out of the Second World War feeling we could accomplish whatever we set our minds to. We dreamed great dreams, educated ourselves and struggled to bring realization of these dreams. We believed in ourselves and we believed in our country. We now face a time when millions of people do not believe in themselves, and have abandoned efforts to dream and pursue their dreams. They have turned their futures over to a government which can never give them what they can give themselves. In the process, they have abandoned any thoughts of using their own potential to be a blessing to this great nation.

In the movie, "Joan of Arc," Ingrid Bergman said to those who were so mistaken about religion, "What you need is faith in God. When you have that, you will have faith in yourself." If we are to restore the greatness of our nation, we will have to restore belief in ourselves, which springs most powerfully from recognition of a power greater than ourselves, a power to whom we are responsible for the stewardship of our lives.

The first sentence of the Declaration of Independence includes the words, "...the separate and equal station to which the Laws of Nature and of Nature's God entitle them." In the first sentence of the second paragraph we find, "We hold these truths to be self-evident, that all men are created equal, that they are endowed by their Creator with certain unalienable Rights, that among them are Life, Liberty and pursuit of Happiness."

At the present time, many people are struggling to understand what freedom means, with some having given up the quest for freedom, willingly placing themselves under the control of people who do not understand there is no better life available than the one people build for themselves. Some do not believe in God, and seek to exclude reference to God in all parts of our government. We should respect their right to not believe because that is a part of genuine freedom. Many people, however, make the error of identifying God with a particular religion, and mistakenly think separating government from religion means separating government from God. Failure to recognize our need for the wisdom of God in our legislation and dealings with each other is what makes it possible for us to avoid our responsibility to help make life better for all Americans. Human wisdom makes space for deal-making, discrimination, bribery, lying, stealing, and many other things which are destructive to our life as a nation, but the wisdom of God permits none of this. We are a weak nation when man's wisdom is the basis of our government.

We must make sure the "A-ha" moment is available to all Americans. This may be the toughest job we have. We must encourage and assist people in finding and following their passion for life. It is not available to those who abandon their purpose for living and cast their lot with those in Washington who think they are the source of life for all Americans. All our citizens must have opportunity to build their lives the way they want them built. For this, they will have to realize government cannot give them what they are looking for. Only they can bring realization of their dreams..

Living in freedom removes us from the tyranny of others. We must become masters of our own lives. The United States remains the only nation in the world where we are totally free to determine what our lives will be. All our citizens must learn that we are not a free people if others have to work and give us bread.

WE MUST LEARN TO BE REAL AMERICANS

Traditionally, becoming an American has meant being born here or taking the oath of citizenship. But, becoming **a real American** is not easy. Many people believe it is, but it is not. It involves much more than being born in the 50 states or receiving citizenship through legal immigration. It is more than a name written on a piece of paper and an oath of allegiance.

Becoming a real American is something you earn. It cannot be bestowed upon you by the government or purchased with wealth. Becoming a real American is learning to stand on your own two feet. It is making your way through life without the encumbrances of government or others who wish to limit and control your life. It is doing those things which result in becoming who you want and wish to be. No-one else can do this for you; you have to do it for yourself.

Becoming a real American involves participating in making this a better country for yourself and others, not sitting down and waiting on the "gov'ment" check. It involves becoming productive citizens, not depending on others to give us a piece of bread. It does not involve separating ourselves out into groups distinct from each other with no concern for the welfare of others.

Those of us who have become successful have done so in an environment of freedom and liberty. This has been a great gift of our country. But, the thing many of us have not adequately considered is the fact that, in order for us to be completely free, freedom and liberty must be available for everyone. When my neighbor is not free, I am not totally free. Many of our neighbors have not been free for several reasons. First, there are those who have turned down opportunities to build their lives in freedom, choosing to be victims of others. Then, many have not learned that freedom is available to them individually. Also, there have been teachers and professors who have not taught students to think for themselves, indoctrinating them in forms of government that are replete with subservience. Being a real American brings us to the place where we can reason and think, making our own decisions about what we will do with our lives. This is where many of us who have been productive have a lot of work to do: assisting others in learning to rely on themselves for success.. We have earned our way through the sweat of our brow in an environment of freedom and liberty, but we must better learn how to assist others as they do the same, not doing their work, but empowering them to do what only they can do, earn their own freedom.

CONCLUSION

Productive people in the United States are angry, far more angry than at any time during this writers long years of life. This anger is legitimate, healthy and good because it springs from something which has already deeply hurt us as a nation and is threatening to make us into something that cannot exist under our constitutional form of government. We are now where we are because of the efforts of our elected officials in Washington, both legislators and presidents, to replace those things which have made America the most successful nation in history and the envy of the world with an inferior form of government.

For a long time, productive Americans have been building their lives on what they consider to be best for them, and we have played by the rules. We have chosen to base our lives on what is on the inside of us, with many of us seeing this as a responsibility to the One who made us. We have not asked that someone take care of us, because we fully realize that is our job. As a result, we have been the greatest nation the world has yet seen.

We have come to a realization that the politicians in Washington do not want us to be who we were made to be. They want all Americans to build their lives on what they think is best for us. This is nothing other than asking us to build our lives on the wisdom of man, which, as we know, always gets us into a mess of trouble. If we choose to build our lives on what is on the inside of us, we have to begin thinking about the purpose of our lives and the responsibility to be who our Creator made us to be. This is not an easy thing to do, but it is the only way we can find the happiness and fulfillment for which we all strive. When we get serious about this, we come to a realization that we are the only ones who can give us the best that life can offer. Politicians cannot do this, no matter how wise they think they might be.

In order for politicians to do what springs from their wisdom, they have had to abuse and use us to fund and run programs which are not needed, and which have brought the possibility of the demise of our great nation. Many of these programs have resulted in millions of people becoming useless as the "gov"ment" check has taken the place of personal work and achievement. We have come to realize that politicians have done this, not because they think it is good for the citizens of our country, but because it will buy votes and get them reelected.

Politicians have brought us to a precipice where collapse of this greatest of nations is a distinct possibility. The value of our dollar has been steadily declining, last year by 21 percent, and the decline is getting worse every day. Legislation which allowed poor people with no jobs and no resources to repay a mortgage to purchase houses is **THE CAUSE** of the economic problems we now have. Personally, because of this legislation, this writer has lost approximately one-half the value of his home and approximately 40 percent in the value of his retirement savings. With this being repeated millions of times across our country, it is no wonder our collapse is imminent.

Legislators want to blame our economic mess on the fat cats on Wall Street, the banks and mortgage institutions, but the major damage has been done by them. Their legislation opened the floodgates and established the rules that made economic mess an inevitability. Without their legislation, what happened would not have happened. They may point their fingers at other people and institutions, but the buck stops under the dome and in the oval office. Bill Clinton said, after signing legislation authorizing poor people with no jobs and no resources to buy houses, "This will end poverty as we know it." What he should do now is issue another statement in which he tells us how many people this legislation has thrown into poverty. In 2010 alone, more than 10 million people were added to the rolls of those who receive food stamps. This legislation has caused an expansion of poverty where it has never before existed, and that is in the lives of many productive people who have lost jobs because of the failed economy generated by this legislation.

The $800 billion bail-out program was an unmitigated disaster, as has been many of the other things under the present administration. From the beginning, this program made no sense to thinking people, and it has not done what Obama and the democrats said it would do, and it has extracted future tax money from our pockets. It has mortgaged the future of the United States in the biggest way ever, and places us at the mercy of our creditors. When a foreign country (China) owns the Empire State Building, something is bad wrong with how this country is run.

Anger is a healthy, appropriate thing to have in light of what legislators and presidents have done to this country over the last 80 years, taking us down a road never intended by our Founding Fathers. The problem productive people now face is how to handle this anger. We will definitely do something with it because anger is always expressed, either in healthy or unhealthy ways. We must decide if our reaction is healthy or unhealthy, good or bad. The healthy way of dealing with this is to use the ballot box and replace those in Washington who have chosen to lead us where we should not go. The American people will choose to do this in a healthy way because we are interested in what is best for our country as a whole.

Productive Americans are aware that this country can become an even greater nation, but we know the process of becoming greater will take all of us doing our individual parts. So long as people are shoved to the sidelines, becoming only spectators, where many government programs place them, we will fall far short of "Life, Liberty and pursuit of Happiness" for all. We have often struggled with this great vision of those who gave birth to this nation, fighting the Civil War and experiencing many other things in our quest to make the good life available to all. At this time, we productive people must struggle against our own government if we are to restore those things which have allowed us to walk where no other nation has ever walked. Our greatness will continue and grow only if all Americans find our individual way to be who we were made to be. Recognition of our responsibility to a power greater than us, something our Founding Fathers recognized, is a central part of this.

If we use our anger in the right way, we can again feel proud of being **real Americans.**

ABOUT THE AUTHOR

Roger P. Bolton has more than 12 years of formal education and training beyond high school. Among these are a BA degree, Mercer University, Macon, Georgia, a Master of Divinity Degree, Southern Baptist Theological Seminary, Louisville, Kentucky, and several years of clinical training in the mental health field, including individual, marriage and family counseling, and in the areas of domestic violence and alcohol and drug addiction.

His credentials are:
>Ordained Minister
>Certified Pastoral Counselor, AAPC
>Master Addiction Counselor, MAC
>Former Substance Abuse Professional
>Certified Clinical Evaluator
>Certified Treatment Provider

He has worked in administration in two senior colleges, has been Chief Executive Officer of four hospitals, and minister in three churches.

He is married to his first wife, and they have three children and seven grandchildren.

Among his honors are Captain of his basketball team in college and President of the Student Council in graduate school.

His previous books are:
>Just A Little Talk With God, Rev. Roger P. Bolton
>The Debacle In Washington And What We Must Do About It, Ethan Leben (pen name)